An Overwhelming Interference

An Overwhelming Interference

EDWARD KUHLMAN

Foreword by Warren Wiersbe

FLEMING H. REVELL COMPANY
OLD TAPPAN, NEW JERSEY

Scripture quotations in this volume are based on the King James Version of the Bible.

Unless otherwise identified, poems are by the author.

THE LOVE OF GOD   Copyright 1917. Ren. 1945 by Nazarene
F. M. Lehman   Publishing House. Used by permission.

Material from THE JOURNALS OF JIM ELLIOT, copyright © 1978 by Elisabeth Elliot. Published by Fleming H. Revell Company. Used by permission.

Quotation taken from *The Singer* by Calvin Miller. © 1975 by Inter-Varsity Christian Fellowship of the USA and used by permission of InterVarsity Press, Downers Grove, IL 60515.

Quotation from MIRACLE ON THE RIVER KWAI by Ernest Gordon © 1962, 84. Used by permission Tyndale House Publishers, Inc.

Quotation by Henry G. Bosch, from OUR DAILY BREAD, Copyright 1984 by Radio Bible Class, Grand Rapids, Michigan. Used by permission.

"Some Golden Daybreak," by Carl A. Blackmore copyright 1934, Blackmore and Son, © Renewed 1962 by The Rodeheaver Co. (A Div. of WORD, INC.) All Rights Reserved. International Copyright Secured. Used by Permission.

Quotations from *Renewed Day by Day* by A. W. Tozer; Christian Publications, Camp Hill, PA 17011. Used by permission.

"Fortune and Calamity," by Dietrich Bonhoeffer from THE PRAYERS AND POEMS OF DIETRICH BONHOEFFER, by F. Burton Nelson. Copyright © by Covenant Press. Used by permission.

Quotations from POEMS by C. S. Lewis, copyright © 1964 by the Executors of the Estate of C. S. Lewis. Reprinted by permission of Harcourt Brace Jovanovich, Inc.

Quotations from THE PILGRIMS REGRESS by C. S. Lewis © 1943 by C. S. Lewis. Reprinted by permission of Wm. B. Eerdman's Publishing Co.

Library of Congress Cataloging-in-Publication Data

Kuhlman, Edward.
  An overwhelming interference.

  Bibliography: p.
  1. Christian life—1960–   . 2. Kuhlman, Edward.
I. Title.
BV4501.2.K79   1986   248.08′6′0924 [B]   85-28289
ISBN 0-8007-1467-9

TO Keith's
mother,
sisters,
and
grandparents,
who loved him
very much.

... that from the Boy there came
Feelings and emanations—things which were
Light to the sun and music to the wind.
... The ... heart seemed born again. ...
A covenant 'Twill be between us ...
I shall love thee to the last,
And bear thy memory with me to the grave.
Michael
WILLIAM WORDSWORTH

✒ Contents ᖚ

⋖§ Foreword §⋗

There are at least three approaches you can take to writing a book about suffering, death, and the enigma of evil in God's world.

You can read a stack of books, take notes, look up scores of Bible verses, put it all together in an organized way, and send it to the publisher. Several books of this kind have shelf space in my library. They are doctrinally sound, philosophically logical, cold, impersonal, and not very helpful. When you read them, you get the impression that the author never really experienced pain and bereavement. All he did was write a book on the subject, the way a student writes a term paper.

Or you can ignore what others have written and just tell your own story in your own way. This works better than the first approach, because a personal story is always more interesting than an academic treatise. But it has this drawback: When you isolate your story from that great "brotherhood of broken hearts," you lose the enrichment of their experiences. I may be wrong, but to me it seems contradictory for a writer to tell his or her story as though nobody else has ever suffered. The problem of pain is an ancient one, and the "great conversation" on the subject has been going on for a long time. We dare not ignore it.

I'm glad that Ed Kuhlman has chosen the middle way and combined both approaches. This makes *An Overwhelming Interference* a very special book, because the author uses the hearts and minds of other sufferers to help him express and interpret his own pain. No, this book is not an anthology of quotations about suffering and death. Rather, it is a lens that collects rays from many lamps and focuses them on one family's experience of suffering and bereavement.

Be sure to read beneath the surface of this book so that the *truths,* not just the *facts,* penetrate your mind and heart. Yes, it will be painful; but it will be profitable. For me, it was an enriching but agonizing experience to read these pages; it was not enough just to weep—I had to worship as well. But don't suffering and worship often go together? At least, that's what Abraham thought when he took Isaac to the altar: ". . . I and the lad will go yonder and worship . . ." (Genesis 22:6).

God bless you, Edward Kuhlman, for writing this book! What a price you have paid! But I believe that your precious investment will pay rich spiritual dividends in the lives of those who read it. It is already enriching my own life, and I thank you for it. Your sacrifice has not been wasted.

WARREN W. WIERSBE
General Director
Back to the Bible Broadcast
Lincoln, Nebraska

Introduction: Loyalty's Hour

Time alone decides
When the unfathomable thrill
of sudden Event
turns into the fatigue of tormenting Forever,
When the day's late hour, dragging on and on
finally reveals what is meant by misery.
This is when most turn away
bored and disappointed
by calamity gone stale.
This is loyalty's hour.[1]

ꞏ❧ Introduction ❧ꞏ

Each of us, someone has said, has at least one book inside him. And the cynic's response has been: "That's where it should stay." How I wish this one could remain inside me— how I wish it never need be written! Yet it tears at my entrails and screams to be released. I am in birth pangs—groaning in travail to be delivered of the burden within my bowels. The mixed joy and sadness of birth. Intermingled pain and ecstasy.

Without embarrassment, I confess that this book is my "sob story"—of love and pain, of life and death, and of all those human elements of which existence is made. But beyond that, it tells the story of God's dealing with my soul in the crucible of conflict as the events of sorrow came together and crystallized. From this present, painful perspective, I look back on a sincere (but not always guileless) attempt to know God in the midst of a world that often becomes inexplicable in its dealings. My tempered soul, more mature now in its reflections, has shed its naiveté and "Pollyanna" notions of Providence. Gone for me are the sentimentals of a "happily-ever-aftering in

13

Camelot." Kurt Vonnegut's acid remark has become painfully accurate: "Yes, we have no nirvanas."[2]

I do not intend, however, to wallow in the slough of despond. What profit is there, not to mention consolation, in preoccupation with the nasty side of life? But I've learned that the "rose garden" mentality is unrealistic for the serious Christian. At one time I assumed that sorrow and suffering indicated spiritual immaturity. Now I know differently. What I once thought were spiritual defects, I now see as the inescapable, fundamental signs of the believer's battle with evil and the unmistakable endorsement of God's seriousness about our lives and lots.

I have always wanted to write a book. I have had several aborted attempts. This was *not* the book I wanted to write. The great American novel; some literate, theological tome; some comic masterpiece: These would have seemed more suitable to my purposes. Little did I imagine that the first serious effort would be so intensely personal and the bitter fruit of a crushed life. I have always been characterized as the clown prince of rhetoric; the plays on words, the pun, the witty retort—these were my stock-in-trade. Dating back to college days, when I wrote regularly for the paper, my corner invariably dealt with the satirical and the silly. How unpredictable are God's ways and how divinely ironic that He typically casts us in unimagined roles to do His work and relate His doings. But *An Overwhelming Interference* is manifestly a book of a burden, wrung from the heart by the winepress of agony and death. Events, personal and overwhelmingly grievous, prompted it. Particularly, I offer it as testimony to God's grace in the face of death—the death of my son . . . my only son . . . my beloved son.

For most people, one event more than all others dramatically reveals who they are. When we survey the landscape of our lives, we observe hills and valleys mixed, montagelike, with some discernible pattern apparent in it all. Above the landscape seems to tower a peak—the ecstasy of our lives. It marks the great watershed of our accomplishments and successes. Typically, we use this as the index of life's achievement.

However, for some a depression of unfathomable magnitude dominates the scene and monstrously dwarfs all else. It seems bottomless and unplumbable, a black hole that draws everything into it, compressing all—a place from which light cannot escape. We dare not venture to near it, nor do we point people to it; yet it, more than the heights, testifies to the worth of our life. Paradoxically its depths provide clear evidence of God's care and concern for us. This monumental blotch on life's landscape says: Here I knew God in an unmistakable way. If you seek a trysting, the sufferer announces, you will find it here—deep, deep in the valley. And this book deals with that trysting place for me. Like Jacob's Peniel—like Joseph's jail—like Paul's prison—all below ground level, it marks the spot of God's grace. The ladder of love abounding with angels is not hinged in heaven, dangling above earth. It reaches to my lowest point—my lowest hell—and offers me the means to elevation in knowing God.

I have not ceased to ask the "why" questions. Although often unanswerable, I have not ignored them. But they are so profoundly personal that Christ alone can respond to them and that in the "still small voice" virtually inaudible except to the soul that hearkens submissively. In this realm I choose to explore and piece together what may be revealed of the pattern of God's working. Admittedly, much of what I say is personal—

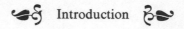

intensely personal at times—but I see a need for such deep sharing. As Paul Tournier has pointed out:

> What is it that makes official or academic speeches so lifeless, like so much chatter? Is it the fact that we take refuge in objectivity, in generalized ideas, taking great care not to express any feelings of a personal nature? Is it not this, for instance, that raises a wall of silence around a person who is dying? . . . We are alone with our deepest preoccupations, when we face sickness, old age, death, all our secret deprivations, all the trials of life; we wonder if there is any meaning in it all. . . .[3]

Because I spend my professional life in academia, I know Tournier's indictment of the sterile, often banal, verbiage that passes for conversation or communication describes its flaws accurately. The practitioners of such verbiage say so little and cover up so much, beclouding vital issues that concern us all. Eager to impress and afraid to disclose, they hide behind the "facile phrase." Like the true hypocrite, they wear masks, like players in a theatrical farce, never venturing into the realm of authenticity.

Candor *is* risky, I realize. Because it costs, many are tempted to take the easier path, turning away from open communication to the hypocrite's mask. For many this means speaking technical jargonese, an excellent cover for their emptiness. But the life-and-death issues of our day cannot afford the luxury of such meaningless language. In avoiding painful honesty, its practitioners hurt both others, who need to share, and themselves, for they need to take part in such actions themselves.

Emotional stability, itself, as Sydney Jourard has pointed out, requires self-disclosure.[4] Phoniness is a major factor in the despair that plagues this generation. We become so fearful of making fools of ourselves that we would rather languish in suicidal depression than slip up. For sanity's sake (and sanctity's), we must summon the courage to express honestly and accurately our experiences, emotions, and beliefs.

The gospel of Jesus Christ gloriously liberates, unlike the slick side-stepping often characteristic of the theological experts, which leaves the shackles still in place. Sermons, dissertations, and other anemic ventures into disclosure more often captivate than liberate. Refreshingly, the Bible never evades fundamental issues or refuses to address the critical issues of life. The Lord Jesus speaks to a Pharisee in nocturnal privacy and to a harlot at noontime. He never wastes words. At the center of the message are the pressing concerns of life. He speaks of the "new birth" and the eternal consequences of it. He tells the woman at the well He can give her the water of life and He will quench the spiritual thirst she had been unable to satisfy. If we are willing to strip away the superficiality and the cloak of conformity and consider life's condition in all its rawness and richness we can be freed and grow in the glorious liberty of the sons of God.

I have never been a particularly public person. For me emotions and feelings beneath surface level have always felt more comfortable. Mature Christians, I have assumed, with stoic resignation put on a happy face, or at least an expressionless one. Still I remain somewhat reluctant to "bare my soul," except to the few confidants whom I trust. However, I am learning that there is a legitimate sharing of deep hurts and sorrows (as well as joys). It is the stuff of human discourse. "Man is born unto trouble . . . ," Job reminds us, and we are assured that it comes to us all.

My recent involvements with people and with a wide range of readings support my belief that *pain* is the fundamental human predicament. No one escapes life without experiencing pain, although many become preoccupied with attempts to alleviate it. Pain is the overriding, inexplicable condition of life. Why must it be? W. E. Sangster wisely noted that "death is not the deepest mystery. We all must die. But pain . . . !"[5] It is the touchstone of our lives. In this "trysting place" heaven and earth meet. Here we meet each other in humanity, and more important, God meets us. As C. S. Lewis has said: "God whispers to us in our pleasures . . . but shouts in our pains."[6]

In this book I propose a painful odyssey. I will honestly relate experiences which to me have been the most painful of my life. If one compares it to a voyage, this is certainly not a pleasure cruise. Instead I have chronicled a stormy assault by the "tempestuous seas" of pain upon this frail vessel of my soul. That may sound slightly melodramatic, but I venture that anyone who has gone through "the valley of the shadow of death" will not think it so. Metaphors, analogies, and examples fall far short of the event, and at best these attempts to translate into word pictures seem feeble.

I have read reams of literature dealing with struggle and survival, pain and Providence, agony and eternity. In fact, for me, the last several years have been a prolonged involvement with these themes. I have read much prison-internment literature, involving lives of people who have struggled through and have survived internment camp experiences. I have been amazed at their resilience. *How could they do it?* I asked myself. More significantly, I have marveled at the strength they have acquired through it all. This theme of struggle and agony has captivated me. I read the prison letters of the apostle Paul and see the increasing growth in "grace and knowledge of Jesus Christ." His life and God-directed hardships only strengthen him and his faith in Christ. And his life did not get easier with time. His last prison experience in Rome was remarkably unlike his experience in the jail at Philippi. At Philippi, God delivered him with the miracle of the earthquake as he and Silas sang at midnight. In Rome, on the other hand, there no miraculous intervention freed him, and the loneliness of the desolate dungeon, forsaken by Demas, seems an inauspicious way for Paul to end. Yet his victorious declaration to Timothy is that "he has fought the good fight" and the time of his departure (setting sail) is at hand.

Time fails to tell of Corrie ten Boom, Alexander Solzhenitsyn, Dietrich Bonhoeffer, and others who have suffered prison privation and have written of the triumph of God's grace in such circumstances. It seems that in the context of struggle with life's harsh and often unfair realities, God meets us. The overshadowing presence of Christ keenly manifests itself in our pain. And iron bars and barren cells do not necessarily make prisons. If stone walls do not a prison make or iron bars a cage, then their presence need not precondition imprisonment. The places in life where privation and pain come to us are prisons as real as any made of material things. The grace of our Lord Jesus Christ becomes evident there. The sorrow that isolates us from human support is the opportunity for fresh revelations from the Almighty God.

On this note I dare to share something of my soul with you. Death is not easy to talk about until it touches your life and bares your soul. Soul baring is soul sharing. Like subterranean springs ready to spew forth, geyserlike, disclosure caused by death's shattering sensations and seismic shock waves erupts eagerly. God reveals Himself to us, and only through His revelation do we know Him. Until that occurs, everything remains conjecture—mere guesswork. Can two walk together unless they be agreed? Agreement occurs when the common core of our souls' longings have struck sympathetically. The vibrations create a consonance—a harmony—an empathy. We are mutually involved. Far too many things in life separate us. Sorrow is the common bond. Come share sorrow with me. Christ, the Lord, shares ours together. "Surely he hath borne our griefs, and carried our sorrows . . ." (Isaiah 53:4). He does not "turn away bored and disappointed." His is "loyalty's hour."

1

An Overwhelming Interference

"Things have come to a pretty pass," said a famous Englishman testily, "when religion is permitted to interfere with our private lives...." Had he never heard of Stephen? or Paul? or Peter? Had he never thought about the millions who followed Christ cheerfully to violent death, sudden or lingering, because they did allow their religion to interfere with their private lives?

... One picture of a Christian is a man carrying a cross: "If any man will come after me, let him deny himself, and take up his cross, and follow me." The man with the cross no longer controls his destiny; he lost control when he picked up his cross. That cross immediately became to him an all absorbing interest, an overwhelming interference.[1]

21

~§ 1 §~

About a month after my son's sixteenth birthday, we scheduled what we assumed would be a routine physical examination. Because Keith was applying for a driver's permit, he needed a physician's report of health. He stood on the verge of young manhood, making the transition from child to adult. The driver's license symbolized that transition—one of the critical steps in the rites of passage for adolescents in American society. He looked forward to a bit more mobility and independence. For years, I had chauffeured him to all activities in the community and at school and church. His involvement in the school bands and orchestra alone involved an elaborate scheduling procedure.

Several weeks before the examination, Keith had complained mildly about a pain and hardness in his abdomen. He didn't make an issue of it or fuss about it, but told us it was becoming an annoyance. I assured him I would have the doctor look at it. In retrospect, of course, we now see a host of symptoms associated with the diagnosis, but at the time, little did we know what monstrous disorder grew within him.

After the examination the doctor asked to see me and ushered me into his office. His face was somber and his eyes were moist. He talked slowly, softly, compassionately.

"Your son has a serious problem," he said. "There's a growth in his abdomen—a mass—a large mass."

I saw him probe my face for a response.

"What exactly does that mean?" I responded cautiously. My physical reaction included a sense of sickness—a mildly nauseous feeling.

"I can't be certain of the exact nature of the mass, but it is large. And it needs immediate attention."

"A mass? What do you mean by *a mass?*"

"It's an abdominal growth—a massive growth—a tumor."

Tumor! *Mass* was much more euphemistic, but *tumor.* . . . The word was one of the most frightening in my limited medical vocabulary. *Tumor* and *cancer* went together in my mind. I sought to make all sorts of associations. In disbelief, I rejected what seemed to be the logical connection.

"Cancer?" I asked incredulously.

"We'll need additional tests to determine whether it's malignant. But it's a large mass—very large."

In that moment, my well-constructed world began to splinter into myriad pieces. Like a pane of glass shattered by a pebble, the fractures fanning out from the hole, I felt an overwhelming sense of unreality. *This can't be true! This is not happening! It's impossible that I'm hearing this!* My son, whom I loved as my soul, might have cancer. *This only happens in movies and books and newspaper articles.* It is something that is never a fact of *life.* Certainly never a fact of one's *own* life! *These things just do not happen. Not to secure, content families such as ours!*

The doctor said he would make arrangements for the tests,

insisting that they be scheduled immediately. With a few phone calls, he had arranged an ultrasound and a CAT scan. It was the last week of school for the year, and Keith was eager to attend those remaining days of classes, wanting to see his friends. He was able to go back for two days, but he missed the last week of school completely.

When the test results came in, they confirmed the worst. The mass was larger than the initial examination indicated, and the doctors scheduled a biopsy. After it, the oncologist diagnosed the ailment: abdominal cancer—neuroblastoma. Untreatable, inoperable, incurable. The prognosis: poor—two months to live!

The only word that could describe my reaction to all of this was *overwhelming*. Like a canopy shrouding me in isolated disbelief, a sense of desolation and despair descended. I felt as if a flood had cascaded from a broken dam and swept me in its flow. The most similar sensation I remembered was being hit by a wave at the seashore, where we used to live. Standing complacently in the ocean, watching the whitecaps gather momentum, unsuspecting, I suddenly turned topsy-turvy, head-over-heels, overwhelmed by the wave—gasping for air and struggling to gain balance. Now my mind reeled, unable to distinguish between the real and the unreal. Acute disbelief—incredulity at the events. I found it impossible to understand, to process this in my mind. My emotions reeled in the agitator of despair.

Before my son went for the biopsy, we sat together in his bedroom. He lay on the bed and I sat on the side of it.

"What did the tests show, Dad? Could it be cancer?"

I wept softly. "Yes, Keith, it could," I murmured. The tears flowed. I sobbed. "Oh, Keith. Oh, Keith," I repeated, convulsed in sorrow.

He sat quietly, saying nothing. "We'll do whatever needs to

be done," I assured him. "Any kind of treatment, we'll get it."

He nodded and smiled faintly.

Keith was admitted to the hospital for the biopsy, which was delayed a day to allow for additional tests. We spent the time together, and I stayed as late that night as the hospital would allow and then returned early in the morning.

Keith was a brave boy. During the extended and seemingly unendurable illness, he behaved courageously. Through that long ordeal I learned something about courage and about courtesy from my sixteen-year-old son. I saw in him a maturity seldom witnessed among older people—indeed, among older *saints.* His attitude and demeanor mirrored the virtue of Christ. Keith was characteristically a modest, unassuming boy. The very qualities I had always wished were mine I now saw embodied in my young son.

When I arrived back at the hospital during the ten-day stay after the biopsy, he was uncomplaining and mildly cheerful. The incision looked like a jagged wire cutting through his abdomen, more than eight inches long. The contents revealed by the surgery were less than promising.

The surgeon stoically related what he had found. The oncologist was a sensitive, supportive man. Together, they told me the results, frankly but sympathetically. The biopsy had confirmed the worst: a mass of cancerous tissue pressing against the vital organs and inextricably entwined in the nerves. Surgical removal was out of the question. The bowels, bladder, and kidneys were affected.

"How long does he have to live?" I asked, hoping for a year or two. I was unprepared for the reply.

"A month—perhaps two!"

When the summer ends, he'll not be here, I thought in a moment of quick reflection. My eyes teared. So did the physicians'. The incredible, hollow feeling of despair drained me of emotion at the moment. Mentally baffled and dazed, I tried to piece together exactly what they had said and what would happen. The frightening finality. Terminal illness! How absolutely terrifying! It was all so abrupt and conclusive. The irretrievable process of death had begun. The specter of life ebbing away in painful debilitation floated across my mind; the ravenous torture of cancer would eventually kill my son!

A single word throbbed in my brain: *overwhelmed*. Whatever the word conveys, it was the only one I could seize. A floodgate opened, catching me in the maelstrom of mixed emotions. I felt hollow, yet filled with a seething cauldron of confused ideas. Still numb, yet I was on fire with rage at the unreality of impending death. The sensations that bombarded me like atoms unleashed in fission were incapable of control. I wept. I groaned inaudibly. My body, my viscera, in union, constricted and ached. From somewhere within me, in previously untapped areas of my being, sensations erupted, and like a geyser convulsing, the substance of my soul cascaded into the hollow places.

Instinctively, my thoughts went to Scripture for help. Where else but to the bedrock of my belief could I seek support? To the Psalms I went. Those ancient songs, some dirgelike, have given comfort for generations. Many from the pen of David, the shepherd-sovereign, have expressed sentiments experienced in the turmoil of pain and death. The sweet singer, close to God's heart, himself knew the anguish that overwhelms.

> My heart is sore pained within me: and the terrors of
> death are fallen upon me. Fearfulness and trembling

are come upon me, and horror hath overwhelmed me.

Psalms 55:4, 5

The horror of death! The unthinkable agony of losing my son. I shuddered as I saw the unimaginable happening. I cried out to God.

Hear my cry, O God; attend unto my prayer. . . . my heart is overwhelmed.

Psalms 61:1, 2

. . . My spirit was overwhelmed.

Psalms 77:3

. . . The waters had overwhelmed us, the stream had gone over our soul.

Psalms 124:4

I poured out my complaint before him; I shewed before him my trouble. When my spirit was overwhelmed within me. . . .

Psalms 142:2, 3

Therefore is my spirit overwhelmed within me; my heart within me is desolate.

Psalms 143:4

My heart was breaking; my spirit was vexed; my soul was agonizing; my body ached and ached. My immediate reactions were to my own grief. In so unbelievably devastating a situation, I could not, at first, see the impact on others. The mystery of one's own consciousness obscures all other considerations at times like these. Within oneself exists a connection so profoundly subjective that external realities fade into insignificance. The depths of being are plumbed. The heart and the spirit, of which David writes, become more than mere abstractions. One's very viscera throbs with the anguish of hurt.

Keith lay in the hospital bed, subdued and quiet. He had always been a reserved and unassuming person. Not that he was shy or lacked warmth or spontaneity, but by nature he willingly took the inconspicuous spot.

"I talked with the doctor," I said hesitantly. Keith's eyes appeared soft and moist.

"What did he say?" my child asked gently.

"There's nothing they can do for you. I'm sorry, my son. So sorry." The tears gushed. My cheeks became wet as I wept without embarrassment or shame. "O Jesus, dear Jesus," I pleaded. "Give Your grace. Be near, O Lord. Be very near to Keith—to us."

Over and over again, I said the words—words of petition, pleading out loud, unapologetically, asking God to grant immediate grace.

"How long do they say I have to live?" Keith asked.

My whole body heaved, tears streamed down my face, my voice quivered with grief. "They say the summer," I answered, sobbing. "We have the summer."

For the first time in my life, I saw my son's cheerful, trusting countenance fall. "I don't want to die, Dad," he said mournfully. "I don't want to die. I want to live and be with you and with Mom and the girls. Why do I have to die? I don't want to die."

I held him tightly, and together, our bodies embraced and our souls bonded, we clung to each other and wept. Is there any greater intimacy than that of sorrow? Do feelings ever explore the full depths of being until the unimaginable grief of separation confronts us? For sixteen years I had known my son. I had been responsible for his birth. He had come from my own loins. He had known no life apart from me. He never became independent of me. Not only had I fathered him, we had become virtually inseparable. The longest time we had ever been apart was for three weeks, and he had never been separated from his mother during his lifetime for a period of more than two weeks. I could not conceive of my life apart from him now, nor could I bear the thought of it. Of course, I knew that I had had an existence before he was born and a life independent of him then. But I was *now* unable to define myself apart from him. My personal identity had redefined itself since his birth. I *now* saw myself as a parent—a father—one who had given my nature to another. To lose him, I knew, would reduce me in some horrible, inexplicable way. Every decision I had made in the last sixteen years was never made without considering him. How could I ever make plans or decisions independent of him? Suddenly the alarming reality confronted me that soon we would be separated in this life.

Keith had a great deal of difficulty recovering from the surgery. His organs did not respond or reactivate immediately, and his stay in the hospital was prolonged. He lay there with a tube inserted through his nose, irritating his throat and draining the horrid fluid from his stomach. It was a day of relief when he was able to have the tube removed and his bowels began to function normally again. We took daily walks through the hospital corridors, attached as he was to the IV machine, with its irritating beeping when the power supply became disturbed. Keith had lost a lot of weight during his hospital stay. His lean frame was noticeably thinner when we finally wheeled him to the elevator and out to the car on the day when he was discharged.

"You're going home today, my boy," I said joyfully to him. He looked at me, his eyes pleading for reassurance. "Home to die, Dad."

My wife and I had decided and had emphatically declared that we would attend to his needs at home. He would not remain in or return to the hospital. Keith was right—home to die!

Even then we hoped the prognosis would not be fulfilled. We prayed that God would grant life. We had no desire to see our son die. Clutching hope, feverishly we prayed that God would grant a stay—that the seemingly irreversible situation would miraculously alter. Until the moment Keith died, we never lost sight of that. We trusted in God's wisdom and had resolved, as painful as the prospect was, to let the Lord do "what seemeth good to Him." But we "hoped against hope" and asked the Lord, repeatedly, incessantly, if He would raise up Keith. God chose not to do so.

Truly one cannot understand the intensity and pain of another's grief. Even if we pass through similar circumstances, we know only our own experiences. We can surely empathize with another person to the extent that we share common experiences. However, in the final analysis, in the inner sanctum of our unreachable being, we bear alone the burden of our grief. *Alone*—the mute monosyllable of a silent isolation. The world outside became a fuzzy, undefinable void, and the inner world of my soul was hollow. *Overwhelmed—overwhelmed—overwhelmed.*

When we choose to love someone (for love always requires a choice), we lay ourselves open to pain. The nerves of affection become sensitized in a way previously unknown. The process of pain (for it is seldom a single, once-for-all act) plays with feelings, and they are the hardest to deal with. C. S. Lewis experienced this enigma when he lost his wife.

> Feelings, and feelings and feelings. . . . Of course, it is different when the thing happens to oneself, not to others, and in reality, not in imagination. Yes; but should it, for a sane man make quite such a difference as this. . . . If I had really cared, as I thought I did, about the sorrows of the world, I should not have been so overwhelmed when my own sorrow came. . . . I thought I trusted the rope until it mattered to me whether it would bear me. Now it matters. . . .[2]

One day, shortly after bringing Keith home from the hospital, I read a devotional book by A. W. Tozer, a godly man whom I had always held in high esteem. I turned to the devotional thought that day rather randomly. God's timing is never in error. Tozer's thoughts dealt with the cross, and he said:

> The man with the cross no longer controls his destiny; he lost control when he picked up his cross. That cross immediately became to him an all-absorbing interest, an overwhelming interference.

In the life of the committed believer, God holds every option. He allows us to withhold nothing and no one from Him. Holy quests and tidy routines equally are subject to His recall and change. How often had I declared to God, in all sincerity, that I wanted His best. I was willing, I had said in moments of ecstatic glory, to let Him have full control over my life and over everything that was mine. Little did I know what this would involve! Would I now commit to Him? Could I honestly say as Paul said: "... I know whom I have believed, and am persuaded that he is able to keep that which I have committed unto him against that day"? (2 Timothy 1:12.)

God had touched *the* tender spot—the tenderest spot. Nothing was more important to me than my family. Career, success, fame, finances—all I had considered trifles. Any of them, I would in all honesty have eagerly parted with. God may take any of them at any time. But to touch my family—to touch the son whom I so earnestly loved—was to touch the apple of my eye. Would I let God interfere?

Only at these times does commitment mean anything. When things are going well and true faith brings, at worst, minor annoyances, commitment to Christ comes easily. It is welcome. Glibly the phrases flow. Vows are made unthinkingly. All sorts of wild, fanciful endeavors for God are promised. Now, called upon to let God interfere with my life, could I submit? When the cross of Christ, which I was bidden to take up, intruded upon the vital issue of my life, would I willingly say: "Not my will but Thy will be done?"

I now walked with Abraham. Brothers under the skin were we, both asked to take our sons, our only sons, our sons whom we loved, and let them be sacrifices. Would I climb my Mount Moriah? *Sincerity* is a word—a mere word, unless it calls for sacrifice. Love is devoid of meaning if there is no demand upon it—if there is no giving. Could I make what for me became the ultimate choice?

Repeatedly throughout the Scriptures, saints are called upon to make sacrifices. The Bible remains a meaningless book unless we clearly understand that word *sacrifice*. Its message strains credulity until the keen awareness dawns that from beginning to end in God's Word, there is a call, a cosmic call to sacrifice. God Himself is the initiator. God Himself, before the foundation of the world, in that uncharted eternity before man and time, decided He would sacrifice. And in this realm of time, God's Son came to do—to be—that very sacrifice. Hence, the pages of Scripture glow with the red ashes of sacrifice, and from Eden's despoiled garden, where animal skins clothe transgressors to eternity's sublime habitation, where the redeemed join in adoration to the "Lamb slain before the foundation of the world," sacrifice breaks forth as the overwhelming theme.

God is the God of intrusions. Just when life has settled comfortably into a pleasant routine, the summons comes. To Abraham, comfortably ensconced in Ur of the Chaldees, comes the summons to go to a country God would show him. Throughout his life, Abraham knew God to be the "divine Interrupter," who directed sovereignly although never capriciously. God's decrees are all ever under His benign sovereign control, and He never wills or does anything except according to His good pleasure. All things from Him bring the clear, unmistakable, and unchangeable benefits of eternity to His children.

I imagine the children of Israel were aroused by the cloud's movement when they felt most comfortable and settled. The divine initiative is the divine imperative. Unlike the deities of pagan literature and lore, spur-of-the-moment indulgences never prompt our Lord. His own character and nature—which, we are reminded by the apostle who lay on Jesus' bosom, are love—dictate God's directions.

The "who's who" in the hall of faith in Hebrews 11 lists

God's chosen ones whose faith was always linked to interruption. God interferes at will—though never at whim. Paul reminds Timothy that as "a good soldier of Jesus Christ" he is called upon to please the One who has recruited him, and he must be ready to respond to any summons to service. The civilian's life may permit the luxury of routine and control, but never the soldier's. The Christian is a combatant. We who have taken up Christ's cross have enlisted in a conflict—one of cosmic proportions and consequences. Jesus Christ, whom we rightly call Lord and Master, has the prerogative of interference in our lives. When the interference overwhelms, it manifests the nature of the purity of our commitment.

I was to learn firsthand, in a profoundly personal way, whether declared commitment to Christ was simply empty verbiage, "vacuous verbosity," or whether it had substance to it. Still I learn. I cannot say with certainty whether the refiner's fire has produced any gold for God, as Geoffrey Bull has so aptly put it.[3] Often, during the ordeal of my son's death, the fears that I would be found wanting, that the balances of bereavement would come up with a featherweight, terrorized me. When the furnace's intensity increased seven times, I felt I would be consumed and that only impurities would surface during the smelting of my soul.

Joe Bayly tells of an incident that happened while he helped get a camp ready for the summer program. A young man ran into the kitchen, holding his hand, pained because he had struck his thumb with a hammer. One of the well-meaning women in the kitchen cried, "Praise the Lord." Bayly, who had lost three children to death, knew that that was the wrong thing to say. He confessed that he did not, that he could not, praise the Lord when his own children were taken.[4]

When the doctors confirmed my son's diagnosis, some gave me similar advice. I became nauseous. God is to be praised, that I know. But I did not *feel* like praising Him then, nor could I come close to anything so radiant. Jesus, at the tomb of Lazarus, groaned and cried. Never did He tell Mary or Martha to praise the Lord. Instead He exhorted them to believe. Overwhelmed by fears and tears, I *willed* to have faith. In the horrible anguish and inner desolation, I *determined* to believe. In my feeble, fragmented being, I would utter, inaudibly, half-heartedly, but meaningfully, the words: "Lord, I believe . . . help. . . ."

~~§ 2 §~~

Soul Sorrow

My soul is exceedingly sorrowful, even unto
death . . .

Matthew 26:38

What broke your heart? . . . Where do you see love
perfected? . . . where the crippled child lies in the
sick bed, pale and wan, unable to help himself.
There the noblest fruits of love ripen and yield re-
freshment. The father comes close to the little sufferer . . . and the mother is nigh all the time to
sympathize. . . . So brokenness attracts God.[1]

ᵈᵍ 2 ᵍᵈ

"Cancer, and cancer, and cancer. My mother, my father, my wife. I wonder who is next in the queue."[2] C. S. Lewis asked. And I answer now: *my* son! Keith, my *only* son! He has cancer. I know, of course, a host of other people have it, too, and daily the death toll mounts. The obituaries, invariably, include someone whose death was caused by cancer. But at the point of my own grief, they seemed only names. I read with sadness about them and was touched but still, they remained, to me, only names. Does it matter of what we die? We all will die. The inevitable fate of all mankind! The death we must die. Does it matter, therefore, what is the number-one cause of death? When reminded that heart disease and cancer were the greatest causes of death, social historian William I. Thompson replied: "What would you prefer be the greatest cause? What indeed? Old age? Nevertheless, it brings death."

Cancer is ubiquitous. As a nurse friend of ours who works with cancer patients remarked: "I think the whole world has cancer!" And it does. Carcinogens prevail, the experts tell us, in everything we eat and in the air we breathe. They are inescapable. But death by cancer is cruel. As it devours children and young people it shows forth its nature. Harshly it devoured our son, ravaging his body, and we saw a four-month-long erosion of his flesh. The supple, lean physique of a teenager on the threshold of adulthood was devoured from within. The monstrous abnormality—the aberration of cells gone wild—consumed that body.

I was present when Keith was born. For the births of my daughters, I arrived late at the hospital. They were delivered quickly, less than an hour after my wife arrived in the delivery room. But Keith's birth was an all-day process that eventually required inducement. That day I sat from early morning in anticipation, and when the doctor announced that we had a son, I was beside myself—wild ecstasy. Minutes later, I saw the thin, frail body and heard his pitiful cries. Over a course of sixteen years, I watched that body develop and change. Each passing year brought maturity and delight. The school pictures around the house chronicle the development. The smiling, all-believing face of childhood. The promise and expectation of youth. The increasing self-assurance of adolescence. Each picture with its characteristic smile or grin—each picture but the last one, taken in his sophomore year—taken just a few months before the cancer diagnosis.

At each stage of development, Keith delighted us. Our inseparable family always did things together. And Keith, the youngest, was such a vital part.

Despite the typical sibling squabbles between Keith and his sisters, the love bond remained strong. The girls would dote on him with a maternal fondness, including him in their schoolgirl games and activities. The 8 mm film we took when we brought him home from the hospital shows them racing excitedly out of the house to greet their baby brother.

Kris was two years older than her brother, but they shared common interests in sports and music. They cheered each other on in their softball and Little League games and enjoyed the excitement of baseball. They played together in the high school marching band, and as Friday-night football games approached, they talked excitedly about the routines they would perform and the band competitions in which they were involved. Their love for music drew them together, and they encouraged each other when they competed for chairs in the county and district bands. They both succeeded and won places in both competitions.

Keith's trumpet, silent in its case, mutely reminds us of the melody they made together. "I not only lost a brother," Kris remarked after Keith's death, "I lost my best friend." As a final tribute to him, Kris played his favorite movie theme at Keith's memorial service:

> Bring me my bow of burning gold,
> Bring me my arrows of desire;
> Bring me my spear—O clouds, unfold!
> Bring me my Chariots of Fire. . . .[3]

Kerry had recently begun to appreciate her brother's wry sense of humor. When she returned home from college, she would "crack up" at his stories about school and the witty way he would parody his teachers. Kerry had been involved in dramatics and speech competitions, and Keith asked her advice about a persuasive speech he had to give for one of his classes. He was preparing to speak on the topic, "The Value of a Marching Band."

"Be dramatic," Kerry advised him. "I know that teacher well. Dress up in your band uniform. Speak with conviction. She'll love it!"

Keith took her advice. He wore his band uniform, carried his trumpet, and extolled the virtues of the school's marching band. He received the highest grade in the class.

Keith was always playful with his mother. As he grew older and taller, he took delight that he could tower over her, and when he reached six feet, he dwarfed her.

"Don't worry, Mom," he would say laughingly. "Your little boy will always take care of you."

She knew he would. How reassuring to my wife to know that, if something ever happened to me, Keith would be there. After Keith's birth she had ended her teaching career to devote her time to him and our daughters. It strained the finances, but we knew it was important for her to be home with them. During the time Keith was growing up and was in school, she was always there when he came home, and she was available when he needed her. He'd hop off the school bus, race to the house, and head straight for the kitchen, to devour the freshly baked cookies in a gulp.

"You're the best cook ever, Mom," he'd exclaim as he gave her a hug.

There are no more hugs and the boyish grin is gone. What prospects remain for a mother whose only son is gone? Women who have lost their husbands are called widows. Children who have lost their parents are called orphans. But what do you call a mother who has lost her only son?

Always the gentleman, Keith added the missing ingredient to the previously boyless home. I knew him all so well. Daughters are a father's darlings. But a son assures the future—the continuation of the family name. Some things within me, which had lain dormant over the years, he brought to the surface. His spontaneous affection kindled the spark within me and in others. His unabashed trust and child faith in his father thawed the frozen exterior and let some of the warmth of my soul penetrate. Even as a teenager, he was unashamed to show affection. Soon, I knew, he would be gone! Would I retreat? Would I crawl back into my cloistered self?

I echoed the words of C. S. Lewis:

> Oh, God, God why did you take such trouble to force this creature out of its shell if it is now doomed to crawl back—to be sucked back—into it?[4]

Sorrow is overwhelming at times like these. So glibly, we say, "I'm sorry." But the chasm between being sorry and experiencing sorrow remains unbridgeable. Even the bright sunny days of summer seemed shrouded in gloom. I viewed everything through the fog of my own frightening despair. My heart was breaking. Jeremiah, the prophet of the broken heart, the weeping prophet, was my kinsman.

> Is it nothing to you, all ye that pass by? behold, and see if there be any sorrow like unto my sorrow....
> Lamentations 1:12

The world seemed so utterly indifferent to my experience. I remember riding to the hospital early that June morning as the cars whizzed by. A Jeep with its top down and sides off pulled alongside at a traffic light. The radio blared. I felt indignant. I wanted to stand up and scream. *Have you no decency? Have you no compassion?* I cried within myself. *Is it nothing to you that my son is in the hospital dying? Is it nothing to you?*

Was there that kind of insensitivity when our blessed Lord hung on the cross? Did a callous crowd pass indifferently, oblivious to the crisis of history? The sorrowing Savior, giving His life for the sins of the world, dying for the very ones who put him there, and for the most part they ignored Him. Or at best, He became the object of idle curiosity. The perpetrators of that "deed most foul" wrung their hands gleefully, content that at last they had dealt with the "Interferer." But the populace, as it has remained to this day, was generally indifferent. Christ seemed simply another victim that day, one among three, and for their part, they were too preoccupied with their own mundane concerns.

Anger tinged my sorrow—a confused, undifferentiated emotion. Was I angry at God? I honestly did not know. I told myself that I was not. I felt angry at my own helplessness. I was no longer in control. The one who meant more to me than life itself slipped beyond my grasp as I watched, powerless to do anything. If we have a course of action available, we feel that the situation has hope. As long as we can press a lever or turn a handle or manipulate something, we exert some power. Is there any feeling so sickening, so despairing, as the feeling of being out of control?

I had concluded a series of studies at a local church. For four successive Sunday mornings, I had spoken on the life of Jacob, whom I had characterized as a model of dependence. In the studies I had tried to show how Jacob had become progressively more responsive to God and less inclined to trust himself. *Jacob*—the name itself conjures up an image of one-upsmanship, deceit, self-reliance, chicanery. God dealt with him over a lifetime, until at the end, we find Jacob "worshipping, leaning upon the top of his staff" (Hebrews 11:21). The independent, self-sufficient Jacob learned the lesson of his Jabbock experience. His wrestling match with the angel of the Lord left him permanently lame, and forever after he limped along, halting upon his thigh. He had a visible physical dependency upon God. Geoffrey Bull has put it poetically: "Self reliance is God defiance." The staff upon which Jacob leaned was the crutch that became his identification mark. From a swagger stick of arrogance to a support of humility—the long lesson of dependency.

Had God prepared me for this experience with my own messages? Lord, touch me anywhere in my life, *but* not in my family—not my son! Take whatever pleases You, but this area is off limits. This is my exclusive, private domain. I am preeminently a family man, Lord. I have never sought my identity in any other area of life. Education, career, accomplishment—by these, Lord, I have gained neither notoriety nor reputation. But my family! My world knows me for that. Touch whatever you like, Lord, and with the apostle of the willing heart, I will "count it but dung." But my family, Lord? My son? What of them?

How willing was I to let God have *everything?* Lord of all or not Lord at all! A slogan. A shibboleth. A cliché. Truth is painful. Several years ago an esteemed older faculty member at the college at which I teach gave a chapel message on this theme of the surrendered life. He concluded his talk with that challenging phrase: "Christ is Lord of all, or He is not Lord at all." He left the podium, made his way to the foyer of the auditorium, and then collapsed. He lay on the floor, lifeless. His last words—his last breath. Is Christ Lord of all?

The sorrow of the summer continued unabated. As the

tumor spread throughout Keith's abdomen and pushed against his skin, bulging his flesh in an unsightly mass, his pain increased. In a moment, I would have gladly taken that monstrous thing into myself. Was there no way I could substitute for him? I had always thought the contemplation of one's own death and suffering through it the most painful prospect in life. I now knew the truth. The ultimate sorrow is watching helplessly as your loved one, your "darling" dies in agony. I can't believe that any parent with the slightest affection for his child would not gladly, yea, cheerfully, trade places without a moment's notice or hesitation with the suffering child.

Joseph was the darling of his father, Jacob. The son of Rachel, his beloved wife. Jacob favored him with the coat of many colors. When his other sons returned the coat to Jacob, bloodstained, the father refused to be comforted. ". . . I will go down into the grave unto my son mourning. Thus his father wept for him" (Genesis 37:35). Jacob spent those intervening years in perpetual mourning. During the famine in Canaan, Jacob sent his sons to Egypt to buy food, and Joseph, who had been elevated to premier of the land, met them. When Joseph insisted that the youngest son of Jacob, Benjamin, be brought to him in Egypt, Judah replied: "Now therefore when I come to thy servant my father, and the lad be not with us; seeing that his life is bound up in the lad's life; It shall come to pass when he seeth that the lad is not with us, that he will die . . ." (Genesis 44:30, 31).

My life was *bound up* in the life of my son. Is not the very essence of love simply this: We find it difficult to separate ourselves from the one whom we love. When a man and woman marry, God decrees that they shall be one flesh. Love in such

an intimate relationship manifests itself in that unity, that one-
ness. Cannot this give us a faint notion of the intimacy of and
unity in the Godhead? The Trinity always in perfect harmony,
indivisibly manifesting uniform and undimmed love? The
eternal love relationship among the Trinity—within the Triune
God—expresses itself in the "image of god" in man. The inexplicable capacity and desire for love with someone else seems
to defy human explanation. How could I love? Callused, uncaring me? How could I feel such exquisite tenderness for my
son? This has no explanation within myself. It comes from
God. We love because He first loved. . . . His initiation of love
permits an imperfect, but nevertheless, real reflection of that
love.

Definitions of love prove defective if not dangerous, because
defining love limits it, and true love is limitless. However, it
seems that an indispensable element in love is *giving;* Scripture
does not describe love apart from this act. The classic verse, of
course, is John 3:16: "For God so loved the world, that he gave
his only begotten Son. . . ." I loved my son to the point of being
willing to give anything, even my life (even my soul?) for him.
I sensed, if only slightly, something of the apostle Paul's feelings for Israel when he said: "For I could wish that myself were
accursed from Christ for my brethren, my kinsmen according
to the flesh" (Romans 9:3). An overwhelming compassion
prompted this willingness to pay the supreme price for his
kinsmen. ". . . I have great heaviness and continual sorrow in
my heart," Paul declared (Romans 9:2).

How close did I come to this supreme test of love? Would I
willingly bear the curse to save my son? In sincerity, I believed
I would have. My sorrow, generated by love (a godly sorrow [2
Corinthians 7:10]) was so profound in my inner being that I

would have laid down my life for my son—my friend. There is no greater love than this. Is there? (John 15:13).

The saintly F. B. Meyer has put it so forcefully:

> This is particularly true of love. We use the term for the mysterious affinity between parent and child. . . . It is the strongest factor in our nature, which bridges distance, defies time, triumphs over impassable barriers, and irradiates with golden light the prosaic circumstances of ordinary people. We cannot explain it. We only know that when this passion takes possession of us, it eliminates self, and makes another's interests the pivot of thought and effort and life.[5]

Although we use the term loosely, *love* has to be the explanation for all that happens in this world, and it is the very source of God's motivation. It vividly illustrates His working. Our capacity for love has no natural explanation. The world, of itself, knows much of lust. It elevates aggression and arrogance in the hierarchy of human values. How improbable that love has its origin in human nature, independent of another higher source. God is its origin. The universe is an unsolvable riddle without love. In love, salvation will ultimately prevail.

Sorrow involves pain. Physical pain is real. I remember, when I was a young boy, picking up a basin of hot water from the stove in our house. The basin tipped, and the water scalded my hands. Blisters rose, and I felt the awful agony of those burns for months. I recall wetting cloths and keeping them on my hands and changing them every few moments to get relief. The pain within me as I sorrowed for my son reminded me of that persisting, scalding sensation. Except, for the inner pain I could get no relief. No cold compresses could I apply to that inaccessible spot. Each new day increased the pain. As I was by his side, joining with him in his desperate illness, the sorrow intensified.

One Psalm in the Psalter is unlike any other. A commentator has titled it, "On the Brink of Despair." About Psalm 88, he says: "There is *only one* Psalm like this in the Bible, to intimate the rareness of the experience, but there is one to assure the most desperately afflicted that God will not forsake him. . . ."[6]

> O Lord God of my salvation, I have cried day
>   and night before thee:
> Let my prayer come before Thee: incline thine
>   ear unto my cry;
> For my soul is full of troubles: and my life
>   draweth nigh unto the grave.
> I am counted with them that go down into the
>   pit:
> I am as a man that hath no strength. . . .
> Thou has laid me in the lowest pit, in darkness,
>   in the deeps. . . .
> Mine eye mourneth by reason of affliction:
> Lord, I have called daily upon thee, I have
>   stretched out my hands unto thee.
> Wilt thou shew wonders to the dead? shall the
>   dead arise and praise thee? . . .
> But unto Thee have I cried, O Lord;
> And in the morning shall my prayer prevent
>   thee.
> Lord, why castest thou off my soul? why hidest
>   thou thy face from me?

> I am afflicted and ready to die. . . . while I suf-
> fer thy terrors I am distracted.
> Thy fierce wrath goeth over me; thy terrors
> have cut me off.
> They came round about me daily like water;
> they compassed me about together.
> Lover and friend has thou put far from me, and
> mine acquaintance into darkness.

In the thickness of my sorrow, that Psalm echoed my lament.

I know I was not alone in fearing to lose a precious loved one. Many face this test, as the Bible shows. Epaphroditus is a seldom mentioned name in Scripture, yet he was precious to the apostle Paul. After a prolonged illness, Epaphroditus recovered, and Paul sent him to the Philippian believers. Paul was uncertain whether Epaphroditus would recover from his severe illness, but when he did, Paul rejoiced and admitted that God had been merciful to him. For if Epaphroditus had died, Paul declared that he ". . . should have sorrow upon sorrow" (Philippians 2:27).

The soul feels sorrow. In the inner recesses of my being, I felt an intensity of emotion I had never previously experienced. I was familiar with the stock theological definitions of the soul, and I knew that psychology, for the most part, will not admit of the existence of the soul. Yet in sorrow, I knew in a profound, experiential way what it meant to have a soul—to *be* a soul. That very pivotal point of being, when all else is peeled away, is the bare nerve. The convergence of being and feeling—of consciousness and compassion. I experienced my *soul*.

In the garden as our Lord Jesus anticipated the dread hour of darkness and the inevitable agony of Calvary He said to His disciples, "My soul is exceeding sorrowful unto death" (Mark 14:34). The overwhelming reality that the hour for which He had come into the world had arrived: with all its immensity, the hour of the cosmic crisis when the eternal Son of God would be made sin for mankind and would give Himself as the sacrifice for sin. As He faced the realization He had reached that point the Lord became shrouded in sorrow. In His soul the Lord Jesus experienced the unutterable sorrow that only eternal God, entered in time, could know. He felt He could die. Right there in the garden, the prospect of what awaited Him and the weight of the sorrow it caused His soul seemed unbearable. He would forfeit His life there. Could He, in the anguish and travail of His soul, *endure until* the cross, so that He could endure the cross? Our Lord was "a man of sorrows and acquainted with grief." Man of sorrows, what a name! Only once in the gospels is it ever recorded that Jesus rejoiced. We have no "jolly Jesus" pictured for us in the fourfold revelation of Himself.

I entered my personal garden of Gethsemane. Although "unworthy to be compared" to Christ's sorrows, I nevertheless experienced the crushing of the soul, and it yielded bitter fruit. The winepress of the garden turned tighter and tighter and wrung from my frail shell of a soul drops of life's water turned by sorrow into wine of mourning.

We had taken Keith to a favorite resort town in New Jersey for a few days. Ocean Grove, an historic, old Methodist campground along the central Jersey coast held special meaning for us. My wife and I had lived there for two years after we married, and we returned there many summers. It was filled with memories and nostalgic moments. In its unchanged, unhurried pace, it remained for us for many years a spot to which we could retreat and turn over old and fond feelings and thoughts.

Keith loved the Grove. It was part of our tradition as a family to spend some time there each summer. Keith's condition had become more severe in July, but we promised him we would make a trip back for a few days. We laid a mattress in the back of the station wagon so he would be able to lie down. It made the trip tolerable for him, if not overly enjoyable. The abdominal pain plagued him, but he rode without complaining, trying to make the best of it in his characteristically pleasant manner.

That inconspicuous spot along the majestic Atlantic Ocean was a hallowed place. Keith and I had walked the beach often. He would talk excitedly. His inquiring mind always searched for solutions, asking questions eagerly. I would try to teach him some Greek words from my limited vocabulary, and we would talk about plans for a trip we would take together to Greece. It was a trip we did take—the summer before his illness. We would never take one together again.

I would point to the vast expanse of water. *"Thalassa—* 'sea.'"* He would mimic, *"Thalassa." "Efharisto—*'thank you.'"* Keith caught on quickly. *"Parakalo—*'you're welcome.'"* He liked the rhythmic quality of that word and would say it over and over again like a parrot. *"Parakalo, parakalo, parakalo."*

We would discuss future plans as we meandered leisurely in the bright sun, feeling the cool spray from the ocean. Our trips together were a favorite topic. We talked about England and Greece. We had traveled together to both places. The memories of the times we shared still linger and remain precious.

In Athens, we had climbed to the heights of Mount Lycabettus and surveyed the splendor of that city nightly as the sun was devoured by the Aegean Sea. The whitewashed buildings glistened in brilliance, reflecting the liquid fire. The Acropolis, in the distance, perched haughtily in its favored place, standing regally as it had for millennia, a dazzling spectacle. The mauved-specked Parthenon flaunted itself brazenly in the dwindling summer twilight.

"Just think, Dad, the two of us alone in this city. No one knows us. Completely alone in a country thousands of miles from home. You and me." Keith felt awed by the sights he was seeing as we sat lazily on the wall encircling Mount Lycabettus. He was fascinated that the two of us were separate from all other people that day in that place. Keith was a boy of simple desires but a young man capable of such profound insight and such guileless affection.

On the Fourth of July weekend we made our trip to Ocean Grove. Keith was able to get down to the beach for an hour only one day, but he was unable to walk the boardwalk or play miniature golf, a game he enjoyed so much. The second night, we went out for dinner to a perennial favorite, an Italian restaurant. Before our children were born, my wife and I would have our typical Friday-night spaghetti dinner at "Mom's Kitchen." In those days it was all we could afford on our budget. We ordered dinner, but before the meal arrived, Keith got ill. Nausea was becoming a constant problem. Keith felt unable to eat. He never ate a meal out after that night. We took him home, back to the apartment. The pain intensified that evening. His bowels were blocked, and Keith bowed over with abdominal distress. Two hundred miles away from our physician, we called around seeking emergency treatment and were finally forced to take him to a local hospital. Ironically, it was in this very hospital that he had been born. How were we ever to know that sixteen years later our son would return to the same hospital, to receive treatment, and that three months later, he would die!

We rushed him to the emergency room then sat waiting for service. I importuned the receptionist, telling her that Keith was in severe pain and needed immediate attention. "The computer just went down," she indifferently responded. Next to me, a man with a third-degree burn, with tissue exposed on his arm, told me he had been waiting for over an hour.

"You must do something," I said angrily. "At least, give him something for the pain." Keith was doubled over.

Finally, another attendant ushered me into a back room, and I filled out some papers, while Keith was taken to a small room. We awaited some attention. It seemed hours before a physician arrived. We felt an absolute indifference to our appeals. To me, that air of casualness in the hospital's routine made it a mockery to medicine. Thankfully, this was not to be typical of our experience with hospitals. In fact, this stands out as a dramatic but painful exception.

Keith was eventually given an injection of Demerol and shortly the pain subsided. The attending physician wanted us to admit Keith that night, but I refused. I decided I would rather run the risk of having him with us or taking him back home than that of leaving him there. *How sad,* I thought. *The very place where he had been born shows so little concern for him as he nears death.* Does medicine in its desire to remain objective lose sight of the very vital human factor?

Keith lay still in bed. He slept little that night, for he feared that the slightest movement would aggravate the pain. I knelt by his side. At first, I remained silent, motionless. I watched his face as he stoically resisted expressing pain. That evening began a long litany of nocturnal sorrow—initiation into the mystical fellowship of the select company who meet God in hidden Gethsemanes. For three agonizing months, I witnessed and participated in the drama of death as a young life, heroically, nobly, resolutely refused to capitulate to cowardice. Angels in wonder gazed upon the "dying form" and marveled that faith could be found in so young and fair a flower of God's garden. The cynosure of celestial attention in a small, inconspicuous room, hidden from earth's attention.

I felt distraught and perplexed. The room was dark and just the hint of light cast ghostly shadows in the corner of the room. I drew within myself. Tears trickled down my face, and I muffled a cry to keep from disturbing Keith. The winepress was squeezing. For the first of many nights the jaws of an invisible vise squeezed my inner being. My bowels were near to bursting. "My bowels, my bowels! I am pained at my very heart; my heart maketh a noise in me; I cannot hold my peace, because thou has heard, O my soul . . ." (Jeremiah 4:19).

The many Scriptures that speak of "bowels" wove themselves into a fabric that stretched taut like a drum within me— "bowels of compassion." Gethsemane—how often our Lord retreated to this private place where the sweet smell of grapes scented the air and olives hung in clusters. The press would do its work. Bruised, crushed, and broken, wine and oil would flow. Sweat like great drops of blood, winelike, would be wrung from that blessed brow.

> Beyond midnight until morn
> on the mount called Olivet,
> He prayed
> with groanings unutterable. . . .
> Solitary.

Silhouetted against an ebony sky
knees blistered and bruised. Brow, sweat-
     soaked,
furrowed by the weight of a world at sleep.
He pleads
unnoticed.
The center of celestial attention but
ignored. . . .[7]

Is this what Christ Jesus experienced? Was I entering into that sacred sphere of sorrow? Passionately I prayed for Keith's recovery. I pleaded that God would raise him up and heal him—that his body would reject this malicious intruder, this sapper of life.

I could not contain myself. Like a broken vessel, my frail, earthen frame sobbed. Like Joseph when he saw his brethren, I could not contain myself (Genesis 45:1). Joseph "wept aloud." My sobs broke through the eerie silence. Keith moved his hand slowly and placed it lovingly on my shoulder. "Pray, Dad," he said softly. "Please pray to God to help me."

The years of buried emotion, hidden beneath the coarse crust of self-control, erupted uncontrollably. I thought again of Joseph, compassionate, kind Joseph who in the presence of his brothers (who had sought to kill him years before) wept un-ashamedly. ". . . For his bowels did yearn upon his brother: and he sought where to weep; and he entered into his chamber, and wept there" (Genesis 43:30).

To the "chamber" I often resorted to pray and to weep, in the private place, the intimate place, where the heart allows it-self to be bared. Tears became my meat day and night. It was "up to his chamber . . . much moved," that David wept (2 Samuel 18:33). In the private place of pathos tears and prayers flow together, in the secret spot of the ultimate intimacies. The Song of Solomon so delicately describes the hushed affection of that place. ". . . The king hath brought me into his chambers . . ." (Song of Solomon 1:4). ". . . I held him, and would not let him go, until I had brought him into my mother's house, and into the chamber of her that conceived me" (Song of Solomon 3:4).

In harmony, in empathy (in pathos together), my bowels yearned within me as my son's physical bowels were obstructed. The problem became more acute as the illness progressed. The persistent agony. Doses of Demerol and morphine. Analgesics. But the agony—the agony—the agony. Endless, the agony.

Alone that night, I felt the weight of his pain-filled world press heavily on me. Through the night, kneeling, I prayed and cried. Could it be that I was treading the winepress myself? Had the spotless Lamb passed this path—this *very* path? If so, how much greater His anguish! Bitterness!

Israel journeyed from Egypt after God's masterful redemption, provided by the blood of the Passover Lamb and by the power of God's outstretched hand. As they journeyed, they came to waters. They needed to drink. The long, thirsty trek in the wilderness. Three days and they had no water. The water that awaited them proved to be sour—bitterness. Moses saw a tree and at God's command cast the tree into the bitter waters, and they were made sweet.

When Naomi returned to Bethlehem after a long absence in Moab, she was without a husband or sons. All had died in Moab. What had promised to be an excursion into a land where fortunes would be reversed proved at the last worse than nothing. She returned empty and bitter. She was barely recognizable to her friends, and they asked, "Is this Naomi?" She replied: "Don't call me Naomi [pleasant], call me Mara [bitter], for the Almighty hath dealt very bitterly with me" (Ruth 1:20). God, however, provided in Ruth (Naomi's inseparable daughter-in-law) the link to sweetness. Boaz eventually proved to be the kinsman-redeemer who would bring back the sweet fortunes that seemed at that time so irretrievably lost. From this marriage, the lineage of King David was established and from him, the Greater Son, Jesus Christ.

God again used the musings of F. B. Meyer to calm the turbulence of my life and let me see something of the sweetness that could come.

> Is there some great perplexity in your life? Is there some anxiety about one dearer to you than life, who is drifting beyond your reach? ... Go to the great Kinsman, find Him when you can speak to Him without interruption, tell Him everything. Hand it all over to Him and then go home and sit still. ... Then the bridal bells shall ring out over an accomplished purpose, and your life shall be no more Marah, but Naomi and bitterness shall be swallowed up in blessing.[8]

Our Lord Jesus hung upon the cross surrounded, John's gospel tells us, by three women—three *Marys*. Mary—Mara: The cross held the bitterness of death for Christ. The bitterness of judgment for sin, which He bore for us. He drank the bitter waters of God's wrath as the women looked on with tears of their own. ("The bitter cup, Thou drankest up. . . .") In the garden on Resurrection Day, our Lord appeared to Mary

Magdalen, one of the three who stood by the cross. It was she who recognized Him after He spoke her name so lovingly. The sonorous tones that she knew so well from early days when with a word He liberated her from the seven demons indwelling her.

"Mary," Jesus said, and she instantly recognized his voice. Her response was, *"Rabboni." Master!* From the waters of bitterness came sweetness on that glad morning when Jesus arose.

Oh, how we await the return of the Lord. Oh, how we anticipate that glad Resurrection.[9]

‏‎3‎

Death-Thou
Too Shall Die

Death be not proud, though some have called
    thee
Mighty and dreadfull, for, thou art not soe,
For, those, whom thou think'st, thou dost over-
    throw,
Die not, poore death, nor yet canst thou kill
    mee. . . .
One short sleepe past, wee wake eternally,
And death shall be no more; death, thou shalt
    die.[1]

3

Death is not a friend. Despite the sentiments of some who try to make death's sad stench artificially aromatic, death remains the loathsome enemy. This the Bible declares (1 Corinthians 15:26). Our *last* enemy awaits its own demise at the hands of Him who has conquered death.

At the prospect of my son's death, I felt nothing but revulsion. The process of dying for him was indescribably horrible. I suppose on some heroic occasions a particular death can take on a transcendent quality, and a glory surrounds it. But I found my son's death odious and repulsive. Why could there not be another way to heaven? Why could not we all walk in as Enoch did? Why does not a chariot of fire swoop down and whisk us away triumphantly into the presence of God?

I believed myself alone in thinking this way about death. The sentimentalized views of death rampant today, when many emphasize "death's dignity," seem to carry the day. I read Joe Bayly's views and felt comforted in my own interpretations of death.

> There is something unnatural and grotesque, even
> wrong about death. Death destroys beauty. Violent
> death creates obscenity—tasteless, horrid, raw. We
> cannot beautify death ... we cannot change its foul
> nature.... Shall we deny death and try to make it
> beautiful? A corpse is never beautiful, animal corpse
> or the corpse of man. Death is an offense to beauty;
> no embalmer's art can possibly restore it.[2]

C. S. Lewis, upon the death of his wife, became outraged by
the grim reaper.

> It's hard to have patience with people who say,
> "There is no death," or "Death doesn't matter."
> There is death. And whatever is matters.... She
> died. She is dead. Is the word so difficult to learn?[3]

I have a fierce, defiant hatred for death. (I did not say fear of
death.) When I read the obituary column in the nightly newspaper, I feel my face flushed with anger. When I read of the
senseless waste of human life in war or of the accidental death
of a child, I become livid. A recent newspaper item described
the death of a fifteen-year-old boy who lived in our community. He attended the same high school as my son. He was delivering newspapers early in the morning, before 6:00 A.M.
That bright, energetic, and obviously industrious youth was
struck dead by a trash-collection truck. How unmerciful!
Killed instantly as he rode his bike. An adjoining column in
the same paper described the automobile accident that took the
life of a sixteen-year-old soccer player in a neighboring town.
The list goes on. Mangled bodies and torn lives litter life's
landscape.

Keith's death, apart from the permissive will of Almighty God, can be viewed as nothing less than a morbid tragedy. An innocent, clean-living, God-fearing, talented sixteen-year-old dies an excruciatingly painful death from cancer. He had done nothing. He had not defiled himself. He was guileless, dovelike in his demeanor. Without an enemy, my son was characteristically modest and unassuming. An honor student—a gifted musician—a personable young man struck down and wasted away. Death, at least, is democratic. It takes young and old, rich and poor. All eventually follow it into the shadowed valley. That much credit can be given it. But it is horrible in the extreme.

Why is not death at least courteous enough to come in stages? I asked a friend this question. He looked at me quizzically. Why don't we die and then return and die again? Allow us to go in stages, so that we can accept it better. Or would we? He thought that would be a good idea. But it doesn't happen. Life is a terminal disease! Death is final, and the finality frightens us. We now talk of the departed in the *past* tense! Once done, it is done, never to be repeated. The terminal terrifies us. I think that is the most unacceptable aspect of death. When Keith died, I could no longer relate to him. We had no more communication. It was finished.

My son died in my arms. I had a premonition the evening before that something might happen. The doctor had told us that Keith would lapse into a coma and linger for several days before death overtook him. It did not happen that way. At times Keith seemed so weak that it looked like the end would come soon, but he would revive and regain some strength. I came home from school that Wednesday afternoon. My wife was there with her parents. She, too, sensed that Keith would not last much longer. She had told her parents to come to the house that day, instead of the following one. They arrived in the morning and stayed through the afternoon. Throughout the afternoon and evening, I remained with Keith. He lay in bed quite weak and not too responsive. I stayed by his side and held his hand and prayed. Fervently, passionately, I prayed that God would even then raise him up. I asked that Jesus, the Great Physician, would give him His healing touch. If the Lord were physically present there in that room, I knew He would raise my son—even as He raised Jairus's daughter, even as He had raised Lazarus from the dead and the widow of Nain's son from off the bier. Jesus restored Lazarus to his sisters. The widow's son was restored to his mother. Would not the compassionate Christ restore our son to us? Jesus, had He been physically present there as He had been in Peter's house in Capernaum, would not have left that need unattended. I prayed and wept. We did not talk for a while. I pressed my head near to Keith's as the tears streamed down my face. Faintly, he said: "Dad, I love you. I love you so much." I wept uncontrollably.

Keith revived, almost miraculously, and became a bit more alert that evening. He sat up and ate a few spoonfuls of food. For several days his kidneys had not functioned, and we still believed, unless they resumed their function, he would soon be comatose. Because they weren't working, the waste had begun building up in his blood system. That was the week of the World Series, and although Keith was not an ardent baseball fan, he enjoyed playing and watching it. Especially the Philadelphia Phillies, always his favorite team—how many times we had gone to watch them at the Vet Stadium in Philadelphia! I distinctly remember one day when we visited relatives in Philadelphia. We left to return to our home, near Harrisburg. As we got into the car, Keith pulled his baseball glove from under the seat, where he had hidden it.

"What's that for?" I asked.

Sheepishly, Keith replied, "I thought maybe we might be able to go to the Phillies' game tonight, while we were down this way. Maybe I'll be able to catch a foul ball."

The trusting face, the boyish grin, the absolute unquestioning faith he had in his father's goodness! To the game we went. Keith's last high school marching band performance took place at Vet Stadium. During April his band performed as the pregame entertainment. Late in June I took him to one final game. He sat through the game in spite of his pain. Never would he see another game in person again.

Keith drifted in and out of sleep the last night of his life. He slept fitfully. He lost control of his bowels. He awakened about 2:00 A.M. and didn't sleep again. I sat with him as he grimaced in pain. His lips whitened—an ashen, ghostly white. *He needs to get his color back,* I thought. He told me the abdominal pain was near to being unbearable. I gave him an injection of Demerol, which helped. The nurse stopped by about 7:00 A.M. and gave him another injection. He thanked her. Always the gentleman. Even in the face of death, he remained polite.

He asked me to help him to the bathroom, but when I tried to get him out of the bed, he fell backward.

"Keith, you can't make it. You're too weak," I said softly.

He lay there for a few minutes. "I need to sit up," he told me hoarsely.

I helped him sit on the side of the bed. Holding him tightly, I embraced him. My whole being convulsed in sorrow. I could not, I did not want to, control my tears. "Keith, I love you. My son, my son, I love you," I said.

"I love you, Dad," he answered faintly. "So much."

I held him, embracing the only son I had—ever had—ever known. My very flesh . . . he seemed to be my very soul. Without a warning, Keith tightened in my arms. He gasped. And he was gone. Dead. From my embrace to the embrace of his Heavenly Father. The body that I had seen only minutes after his birth. The body I had watched grow—had bathed and dressed and hugged and admired. The body that had grown and reached the verge of manhood. Now lifeless—now dead.

"Oh, Keith," I sobbed. "My son, my son." I bowed my head. "Dear Lord Jesus, receive the spirit of my dear son. Receive him into Your eternal abode. Receive him lovingly."

For a moment I held the lifeless body close to me and then rested it on the bed. I sat holding his hand; this member that once pulsated with life and energy now turned cold and limp. The eyes, which had danced and sparkled merrily and which had taken in the world eagerly, stared vacantly, sightless. I closed the lids. That emaciated body. Cancer had done its cruel deed and had eaten it away. I called the doctor, who came promptly. As my wife, the doctor, and I stood silently by the bed a hushed reverence enveloped the room. At that obscure point time and eternity had converged. The drama endlessly being acted out since Adam was complete. Another soul had slipped beyond time's boundary. Not long after, the undertaker arrived. As if to cover my pain, the sky quickly clouded over. I went downstairs and sat peering into the gray autumn sky. Streaks of sunlight sliced through the clouds, but soon the sky turned pewter. A soft rain began to fall. Mistlike, the sky wept, too. In the distance, peals of thunder reverberated as the sky darkened and the rain increased, becoming torrential. Lightning brightened the sky. *How unseasonable,* I thought. *Like Golgotha!* The sky turned dark that day as God's *only* Son lay down His life. That Friday in Jerusalem cosmic clouds congealed, and rain tearfully fell; heaven veiled itself. The holy eye shuttered on that sight as the blessed Son of God died.

The undertakers brought the body of my son downstairs and carried it to the hearse. As they left the house the rain stopped abruptly, the clouds dissipated. Streaks of sunlight again filtered through the clouds. The skies cleared rapidly and sunshine radiated. The hearse pulled away. The body of my son was gone.

Death is the great divider, bringing with it the inevitable consequence: separation. God had said to Adam, in the Garden of Eden, "In the day that you eat of the tree, you shall *surely* die." No idle words those. And death has passed upon all men, for all have sinned (Romans 5:12).

On my son's death notice, the cause of death was listed:

Cardiopulmonary arrest—1 minute
Renal Failure—1 week
Neuroblastoma—5 months

That was the medical explanation. The notice could have listed one additional and most critical cause of death, the ultimate cause: SIN. For all of us, our death notices could carry that, too. Sin causes death. Had there been no sin, no one would ever have died. God never intended it. Sin is a monstrosity, an aberration of the most heinous sort. It is a grotesque, bizarre anomaly. "Then when lust hath conceived, it bringeth forth sin: and sin, when it is finished, bringeth forth death" (James 1:15). God has promised that He will abolish death: ". . . and there shall be no more death . . ." (Revelation 21:4). Christ Himself declared that those who believe on Him will experience no second death—no eternal death. "Death is swallowed up in victory." (1 Corinthians 15:54; Isaiah 25:8)

Keith and I were now separated. Physically, we remain apart. His body lies interred, in the ground, undergoing decay. Like all before him, he experiences corruption. He himself is in heaven in the presence of Christ: ". . . To be absent from the body, and to be present with the Lord" (2 Corinthians 5:8). ". . . God is not the God of the dead but of the living" (Matthew 22:32). Death is not desirable. Dying itself holds no virtue. But "to have died" presents us into the incomparable presence of our blessed Savior.[4]

Death means inevitable separation. When Adam sinned, he became separated (and alienated) from God. Adam was separated both from his wife, Eve, and from himself. The work of Satan from the beginning has been the work of separation, his strategy, to divide and conquer. God alone restores and reconciles. His master plan for this world, for the universe (for it has cosmic implications and consequences), is to bring all things together in Christ. "That . . . he might gather together in one all things in Christ, both which are in heaven, and which are on earth; even in him" (Ephesians 1:10). Ultimately and indisputably, God's will prevails, and the great consummation in Christ Jesus will see the restoration of all things. Death divides, but love in Christ unites, reunites, and restores.

How often I long to talk with Keith, to see him, to have his physical presence with me. This response is typical of all who have lost loved ones. I do not wish him back. That would mean selfishly having him continue in suffering. What was the profit in Lazarus's recall from death? Scripture says little of him after his summoning from the tomb, except that he continued in fellowship with the Lord. ". . . Lazarus was one of them that sat at the table with him" (John 12:2). A little poem simply captures our desire to see loved ones who have departed this life.

> A shadow flits before me
> not thou, but like to thee

> Ah Christ, that it were possible
> for one short hour to see
>
> the souls we loved, that they
> might tell us
> what and where they be?[5]

Keith didn't want to die. He would sit longingly through the still hours of the night. "I don't want to die, Dad," he would say. "I want to be with you and Mom and the girls. I want things to continue just the way they are."

My wife would sit by his side as he lay on the bed, and they would talk about the happy times we had had together. They watched a rerun of a television program originally shown near Christmas time. The prospect of not having Keith for Christmas again brought tears to her eyes. Consolingly Keith touched her hand.

"Don't cry, Mom," he said softly. "If you cry, then I have to comfort you. It's all right for Dad to cry with me. We cry together. But when you cry, I feel so helpless. I don't want to see you like this. Everything will be fine."

My wife has always been a woman of strong faith and character, and during the time of Keith's illness, she remained resolute and resilient. In response to his plea, she seldom wept in his presence. She would smile when she sat with him, knowing that soon he would be gone from her. The body to which she had given birth, a difficult birth, would shortly be hidden away in the earth. But the tears she shed sparingly at his bedside would soon flow unhindered when Christmas came, or a trumpet played, or the sweet memories touched her heart.

The music that seemed so pleasant during Keith's lifetime became particularly painful after he died. His sisters could not hear a band rehearsal or listen to a Chuck Mangione recording without feeling deep emotion. Love's bonds that linked us so closely together did not slacken when Keith was gone. These were the things he wanted to continue to be part of.

Death disturbs all routines. It comes discourteously and interferes. Still I get a sickening feeling when I remember the summer months and how I anticipated Keith's impending death. The absolutely unimaginable was happening. I knew people died, but frankly, I never believed *I* would die. Certainly, never for a moment did I believe my young son would die. One always expects death for the *other* person. It would not happen to *me!* But it does. And it did! Abruptly, conclusively, and irreversibly death came and removed my son. No longer can we count him among the living on this earth. All human contacts ceased, and all obligations stopped. That quickly! One last breath! On all forms, we now check the space "deceased." His memory remains for us. The grave marker becomes a mute memorial.

Yet my son lives! He is more alive than he ever was. D. L. Moody, on his deathbed, assured those around him that when he had breathed his last breath, he would be more alive than he had ever been. Earth is a place of death. But heaven—heaven is the grand place of life eternal.

As the Scriptures declare, paradoxically, life comes from death. A different life—a resurrection life. Now that death has entered the world, God has in His grace transmuted it into life. The death, burial, and resurrection of our Lord Jesus Christ testify eloquently and eternally to the glorious victory God has wrought. It is a riddle. The Resurrection of Jesus is the supreme riddle. Samson's riddle refers to that very thing: "Out of the eater came forth meat, and out of the strong came forth sweetness . . ." (Judges 14:14). C. S. Lewis's Aslan, the mighty

Lion slain and resurrected, is a parable about the same truth. ". . . What is sweeter than honey? And what is stronger than a lion? . . ." (Judges 14:18). Christ, the Lion of the tribe of Judah, became the Lamb. "And one of the elders saith unto me, Weep not: behold, the Lion of the tribe of Juda, the Root of David, hath prevailed. . . . And I beheld, and, lo, in the midst of the throne . . . stood a Lamb . . ." (Revelation 5:5, 6). The strong Lion became the weak Lamb crucified. But now He is in resurrected strength. Although He was crucified through weakness, He now lives by the strength of God. From the death on the cross comes the sweetness of life eternal through the Resurrection.

Christ was the "corn of wheat" who fell into the ground and died. He gave His life that we all may be included in the harvest of God's redeemed family. ". . . Except a corn of wheat fall into the ground and die, it abideth alone: but if it die, it bringeth forth much fruit" (John 12:24). Christ has become the firstfruits and assures us that we will share, by faith in Him, in the resurrection harvest.

Keith has died, but from that kernel of wheat of his life, new life comes. The shell that held the old life died and disintegrated, and the new life of the inner man, which is renewed daily, springs forth—the mystery of God's conquering death and resurrection power.

For several years, I have jogged daily along a favorite and familiar route that meanders along back roads and beside cornfields. I have watched the perennial progression of the corn: the newly cultivated fields in early spring, the first detectable green shoots above the ground, soon the blade and then the ear and then the full corn. Just as the old hymn recounts it. In the autumn, the green field gives way to the somber hues of brown and gold. Then the stalks weakly bow in the chilled autumn air. One day, the cornfield appears as a barren spot against a bleak sky. Nothing but stubble remains.

As I jogged along the route in early June and infrequently during the summer, I watched the growth intently. I knew that before that harvest was over, Keith would no longer be with me. With two months to live, he would not outlive the corn in the field. The fragility of life. The annual ritual of planting. The cycle of life. "A time to plant, and a time to pluck up that which is planted. . . . A time to be born and a time to die" (Ecclesiastes 3:2). Keith had been planted. The seed in the womb. He had grown up as "a tender plant." Now, seemingly prematurely, he was being plucked up.

As the fetus lies still in the darkness of the womb, waiting for birth, it knows little of what lies beyond. But for that life outside it is intended. Its intrauterine state is not its destiny. As secure as it appears, no one can live always within the womb. The preliminary stage—a necessary first step—must not be confused with the divine destiny. We do not see the fetus as the ultimate product—the final intention of the union and sperm and egg. Soon, we know, it will be jettisoned into the world beyond, and the new life will exist in a new environment. To live in the womb beyond its time would deform that life. To lock it away in that environment would limit potential and growth. So it is with our earthy life. God created us to enjoy eternal life with Him, and the world of sin and the "body of this death" limit us in fulfilling that intention and enjoyment. The apostle Paul said he was "in a strait betwixt two." He wanted to unburden himself and "depart, and to be with Christ" (Philippians 1:23). He saw his present body of humiliation as a tabernacle soon to be dissolved and he desired the "house not made with hands, eternal in the heavens." He groaned "earnestly desiring to be clothed upon with our house which is from heaven. . . . For we that are in this tabernacle do groan, being burdened: not for that we would be unclothed, but clothed upon, that mortality might be swallowed up of life" (2 Corinthians 5:1, 2, 4). Paul eagerly awaited his own "departure." In both Philippians (1:23) and 2 Timothy (4:6) Paul talks about his "departure." "Departure" (Greek: *analusis*) also translates into the English word *analysis.* Paul awaited his "analysis," the unriddling of life, the final "working out" of his salvation. His unloosing from the shore, the freedom from the restrictions of a mooring, would allow him to launch out onto the broad expanse of God's loving care in Christ Jesus. There he knew he would experience the eternal ecstasy of the new life in the unending realm of God's glorious presence.

When Keith died in my arms, I knew that he entered the place of no restrictions from the infirmities of the flesh. If this were not true, I would have no alternative but to declare life a monstrously cruel joke played upon frail humanity. If this life simply ended all, then life itself is horrid. One finds little consolation in knowing a few fleeting pleasures and fondnesses in this life, if the grave claims all in oblivion. It would be a cosmic farce—the most unconscionable of delusions. If Keith were forever beyond my knowing or affection, I would declare that life had been a sad and sickening tragedy for which there is no excuse and no reason, and I would suspect that sadism was the source. "If in this life *only* we have hope in Christ, we are of all men most miserable" (1 Corinthians 15:19, *italics mine*) is the classic understatement! As C. S. Lewis put it: "You bid for God or no God, for a good God or the cosmic sadist, for eternal life or non-entity. . . ."[6]

But I affirm unequivocally, categorically, unambiguously

that God is good! God is nothing less than, nothing *other* than good. Moses asked God to reveal His *glory* to him on Mount Sinai, and the Word declares that God said, "I will make all my *goodness* pass before thee, and I will proclaim the name of the Lord before thee . . ." (Exodus 33:19, *italics mine*). "And the Lord descended in a cloud, and stood with him there, and proclaimed. . . . The Lord, the Lord God, merciful and gracious, longsuffering, and abundant in goodness and truth" (Exodus 34:5, 6).

Jonah learned that God's greatness is His graciousness and His might is His mercy. Of all the great things mentioned in the book of Jonah (wind, city, and so on), the chronicle never specifically mentions God's greatness. Instead it reveals it in His grace and graciousness to the people of Nineveh. So God manifests His marvelous grace to us. The great work of God in redemption is His goodness poured out upon us.

The Lord Jesus went about "doing good," and the good that He did was "His father's business." God's business is *good* business. When the clouds of despair obscure the sun of God's presence, and when our lives become cluttered with the flotsam and jetsam of the shifting tides of trial, God's promise that these things are for good—for our good—remains unstifled. "And we know that all things work together for good to them that love God, to them who are the called according to his purpose" (Romans 8:28). Joseph said to his brothers who had sold him into slavery: "But as for you, ye thought evil against me; but God meant it unto good . . ." (Genesis 50:20). God transmuted through the alchemy of His mercy the base metal of life's trial into the gold of glory. In my personal anguish, I wondered if, when the crucible of purging had cleared away the dross, any nuggets of gold would remain. "That the trial of your faith, being much more precious than of gold that perisheth, though it be tried with fire, might be found unto praise and honour and glory at the appearing of Jesus Christ" (1 Peter 1:7).

Our lives are not controlled by the hands of fate or the caprice of an uncaring deity remote from our lives. We are not pawns on the cosmic chessboard of an indifferent game player who amuses Himself with our puny lots. Never can this be! The Christian knows, in an uncanny, paradoxical way, that at the time of intense trial God controls and cares.

In the throes of tearful agony, in those heart-wrenching hours of nocturnal sorrow, I knew God was for me. When my world seemed to split in two and I feared for my sanity, I knew that He who watches the sparrow (the most worthless of birds) fall, and He who provided a nest on His altar for the swallow (the most restless of birds) would provide for me. Romans 8:28 was more than a mere cliché to be mouthed mechanically at testimony time. "And we know. . . ."

Instinctively, intuitively, in our being of beings, we know that God works—for good. We know this because we have come to know God. To know God is to know that He will never do anything contrary to His eternal glory and our eternal good. ". . . If God be for us, who can be against us?" (Romans 8:31). Death may separate us from each other, but it can never separate us from the love of Christ. (Romans 8:35, 38, 39). As our Father God may chasten us (Hebrew 12:7), but He never chastises us, because His beloved Son bore our chastisement (Isaiah 53:5). He does not punish His children, but lovingly disciplines and shapes and molds and refines and prunes. The old growth goes. The dross is refined away. As a father pities his children, so the Lord pities those who fear him (Psalms 103:13).

At the human level of understanding, I have trouble achieving the reconciliation of the death of my son and God's working for good. It defies logic. No rational judgment seems to support it. However, there exists a transcendent truth beyond the human, beyond the logical; the intelligence of God works purposefully in love. And one day, we will humbly, and knowing no longer in part, declare that God has done all things well.

4

My Son...
My Son

All this is flashy rhetoric about loving you
I never had a selfless thought since I was born.
I am mercenary and self-seeking through and
    through:
I want God, you, all friends, merely to serve
    my turn.

Peace, re-assurance, pleasure, are the goals I
    seek,
I cannot crawl one inch outside my proper
    skin;
I talk of love—a scholar's parrot may talk
    Greek—

But, self-imprisoned, always end where I
  begin.

Only that now you have taught me (but how
  late) my lack
I see the chasm. And everything you are was
  making
My heart into a bridge by which I might get
  back
from exile, and grow man. And now the bridge
  is breaking.

For this I bless you as the ruins fall. The pains
You give are more precious than all other
  gains.[1]

To do His supreme work of grace within you, He
will take from your heart everything you love most.
Everything you trust will go from you. Piles of ashes
will lie where your most precious treasures used to
be. . . . Then you will learn, probably to your aston-
ishment, that it is possible to live in all good con-
science before God and men and still feel nothing of
the "peace and joy" you hear talked about so much
by immature Christians.[2]

❧ 4 ❧

So writes A. W. Tozer with characteristic candor. Was the loss of my son God's supreme work of grace within me? Could someone so incalculably precious to me be taken and the very taking be an act of God's grace to me? Jim Elliot once wrote: "If it's not of grace, it's not of God." Dare I believe this? I had told God so many times that what I had was His. Was He taking me at my word? Was He now claiming that which I had given to Him?

More than two decades ago my own father died. I never knew him well. He was an alcoholic. I never remember a kind word from him or an affectionate embrace from this hard, cruel man. He was fierce and impulsively violent. Only once did I see him between the time he left us, when I was a child, and the day of his funeral. He came to the wedding of one of my brothers. Looking at me—one of seven sons—he asked: "Which one are you?" When he died, I felt almost no emotion. That evening as I lay in bed, a single tear forced its way from my eye and rolled down my cheek. One tear! A sentimental tribute to the father I never really had.

During the months of my son's illness and after his death, I wept more than I had in the preceding forty-seven years. My son allowed me to be to him the father I had never had, and he was to me—and more—the son I had always wanted to be.

He was *my* son. The *only* son I had. He was not one of many. Single—solitary—one—apart—alone—and there would be no more. No more.

Abraham, the great patriarch, was told one night by God to gaze into the expanse of heaven and number, if he could, the myriad of stars that blanketed the celestial canopy. He of course could not. Later God walked with Abraham along the beach and had him sift the sand through his fingers, and as the grains trickled to the ground God told Abraham to count them. Impossible. The question then posed was: Do you believe Me, Abraham? We are told that years later God commanded Abraham to take his son, Isaac, to Mount Moriah. "And he said, Take now thy son, thine only son Isaac, whom thou lovest, and get thee into the land of Moriah; and offer him there for a burnt offering . . ." (Genesis 22:2). It was no longer a myriad of stars, no longer a multitude of sand, but a single, solitary life—that of his son. Scripture tells us Abraham did what he was commanded, and God now knew that Abraham feared Him.

I had given whatever I had to God. God now decided to take what I gave Him. And He took him in the agony of pain and debilitating cancer. O God, must you touch *the* tender spot? Must you touch *the* apple of my eye?

One day I picked up a small book written by a popular author of Christian literature. I opened the volume at random. At the top of the page were these words: "Take now thy son . . . and offer him there for a burnt offering." It was addressed to me. I recalled those fleeting moments when I entertained thoughts of what God's will might require in my life. I remembered painfully looking at my children and thinking, for a brief, light-speed moment, would God ask me to part with them? As quickly as the thoughts would come, I would dismiss them. No! Never! God does not do that! The son who was the sunshine of my life. We shared sweet fellowship together. He had told me often that he really needed no close friends. It was enough that he had his family. It was enough that I was his father. As he lay dying he said: "Dad, we've always been close, but we've never been closer than we are now." That little blue-eyed, towhead of three—of six or ten—and now sixteen. The golden intimacies of his youth. The cheerful voice. The little songs he would make up. Happy songs about his family. The times he would try to run past me toward the couch to score a touchdown. "Horsey rides" around the house. The nightly ritual of baths and stories. Evening Bible readings and guileless prayers. All these I loved. All these made my feeble life so worthwhile. Now to the world an insignificant, obscure teenager. To me, the reason for life and the proof positive of a gracious, benevolent God.

Jonathan, the faithful son of an arrogant father, loved David as his own soul. Jonathan sacrificially relinquished the kingdom to David. He placed his life in jeopardy and in the process earned the scorn of his father. David, with characteristic pathos, lamented the death of his "soul brother." "I am distressed for thee, my brother Jonathan: very pleasant hast thou been unto me: thy love to me was wonderful, passing the love of women" (2 Samuel 1:26).

I loved Keith as I had never loved anyone. I loved him in a way I had never loved any boy or man. In sonnet and song poets herald the love of a man for a woman and a woman for a man. The intimate, tender love the sexes alone can share. The physical intimacy—the romance of opposites entwined in passion and soft embrace. We celebrate this sweet love. But another love also penetrates the soul. It is the mating of kindred spirits and souls. Keith and I shared that love. During his illness, he talked of all the endearing terms I had used when he was little. He would tell me how good they made him feel, how they reassured him. He told me how he would look at me and feel good inside, how safe and secure he felt when I was near. We shared the joys of present companionship and the prospects of the future. I quite honestly could not conceive of a future without him. I still cannot. The prospect that he will not be near, that as I approach old age he will not be the son by my side, seems incomprehensible.

David heard the news of Absalom's death. Absalom, his wayward son, had conspired to take the kingdom from his own father. But David, preeminently the man of mercy, wept uncontrollably at the news. The man after God's own heart was tenderhearted. When others would rejoice at the death of a traitor son, David mourned.

> And the king was much moved, and went up to the chamber over the gate, and wept: and as he went, thus he said, O my son Absalom, my son, my son Absalom! would God I had died for thee, O Absalom, my son, my son!
>
> 2 Samuel 18:33

One of my contemporaries who has shared similar experience and sorrow wrote of his grief:

But with Jonathan's illness and death, we encountered something too difficult to verbalize. The hurt was too deep, the loss too staggering, the grief too heavy for language. So tears were the main outlet for an internal groaning that was beyond words. . . . I missed Jonathan so. He had been my pride and joy. . . . I felt like I had been struck in the heart with a spear; and the missile once retrieved, had left behind a gaping hole that only he could fill. No one else could take his place—not even God. . . . I didn't want Jonathan to be gone. Hanging on to my grief was a way of hanging on to him.[3]

As a child, I wondered about fathers. My own father, as little as I ever knew him, was harsh and uncaring. He lacked compassion. *Is that what God is like?* I would wonder. *Is this what fathers are intended to be? Are fathers tyrants who rule arbitrarily and mercilessly?* I confess that to this day faint traces of this fear remain. I know now, within myself, that God has permitted me to witness fatherly kindness in my relationship with my son. Had I never had children, had I never had this son, I would have remained solidly convinced that fathers were without feeling, and I would have suspected (although I never would have proclaimed it in public) that God Himself was the same. How could I look at Keith and feel within myself the flush of affection? Doubtless, it came from God—the Father—the One "out of whom every fatherhood in heavens and on earth is named" (Ephesians 3:15, Greek translation). To the Great Initiator, the Supreme Lover, I am eternally indebted for the privilege—the overwhelming and profound passion—to have had my son.

Yet the questions remain. Why has he been taken? Why has the dear Father parted us? Is it better to have loved and lost? In his *Confessions,* Augustine agonizes over the loss of his friend and judges that it is not proper to love humans more than God. But can we, in fact, love God if we know nothing of human love? Does not John, the apostle whom Jesus loved, rightly raise the question: "... For he that loveth not his brother whom he hath seen, how can he love God whom he hath not seen?" (1 John 4:20). Has my love for Keith led me to greater love for God? In loving my son has my capacity for loving God increased? Is the human love a parable of God's love? This kind of love is both rare and risky.

Polite but harmless love causes little upset when the loved one goes. In such cases the marriage vows so glibly said, which presumably attested to devotion, end in perfunctory divorce— and that without emotion. I recall having witnessed the court proceedings of a custody hearing for a couple who had recently divorced. They sat staring daggers at each other, venom dripping from their words. Where they had once vowed commitment, now only epithets of hatred remained. Love is never leisurely in this respect, unless love is so poorly defined that it simply means self-gratification. Love is a fragile commodity. It lays us open to hurt and despair. It renders us vulnerable, and the Goliath's soft spot of our love leaves us open to slings and stones that may leave us in a crumpled heap.

C. S. Lewis describes the dangers of loving:

> To love at all is to be vulnerable. Love anything and your heart will certainly be wrung and possibly be broken. ... The only place outside heaven where you can be perfectly safe from all the dangers and perturbations of love is Hell. ... We shall draw

nearer to God, not by trying to avoid the sufferings inherent in all loves, but by accepting them and offering them to Him ... throwing away all defensive armour. If our hearts need to be broken and if He chooses this as the way in which they should break, so be it.[4]

But what exactly was this "love" that I felt—experienced? Why, among so many people, was Keith alone able to elicit this response from me? Had God designed our lives to be in conjunction, like stellar constellations? Had God infused this relationship with the effulgence that flowed from Himself? Are relationships the fulcrums where God's love has leverage? Can God only move in human lives when "two are agreed"? Has God planted within each of us, reflective of His own image, a personal capacity for a relationship that microscopically, like a mirror, reflects His limitless love? Does the vast variety that abounds in nature testify to the need for plethoric means for God to manifest His unbounded love? To say "God is love," as John declares, cannot simply be a terse aphoristic pronouncement; it exclaims the deepest of all profundities ever uttered by human voice. To say that "God so loved the world that he gave his only begotten Son ..." is to utter the most sublime words ever addressed to human ears.

Viktor Frankl, in his memorable and magnificent writing that chronicles his Nazi prison camp experiences, records startling words that broke upon him one cold, icy morning as he stumbled to his labor for the day:

A thought transfixed me: for the first time in my life
I saw the truth as it is set into song by so many poets,
proclaimed as the final wisdom by so many thinkers.

The truth—that love is the ultimate and highest goal to which man can aspire. Then I grasped the meaning of the greatest secret that human poetry and human thought and belief have to impart. The salvation of man is through love and in love. I understood how a man who has nothing left in this world still may know bliss, be it only for a brief moment, in the contemplation of his beloved. In a position of utter desolation, when man cannot express himself in positive action, when his only achievement may consist in enduring his sufferings in the right way— an honorable way—in such a position man can, through loving contemplation of the image he carries of his beloved, achieve fulfillment.[5]

A particular quartet rendering of a most reassuring hymn helped keep before me the reality of the great love of God in those days of anguish. The record would play over and over, and the words were melodic and tranquil:

> O love that wilt not let me go,
> I rest my weary soul in Thee;
> I give Thee back the life I owe,
> That in Thine ocean's depth its flow
> May richer, fuller be.

The words penned by George Matheson, himself a sufferer, told of God's persistent love. Fragile love—tough love. Love that does not break its links too easily. Eternal love is knotty and strong. My love for Keith was like that. Would I not do anything to save him? To spare him the illness and pain? I thought of Moses' prayer to God that God not obliterate Israel as He had threatened. Moses preferred, unhesitatingly, that he himself "be blotted out," if need be. Paul could wish himself accursed for his brethren's sake. Would I willingly be accursed for my son's sake? I think so. I *know* so! C. S. Lewis, the kinsman of the sorrowing soul, relates his own feelings as he reflected on his wife's death from cancer.

> If I knew that to be eternally divided from H. and eternally forgotten by her would add a greater joy and splendor to her being, of course, I'd say, "Fire ahead." Just as if, on earth, I could have cured her cancer by never seeing her again, I'd have arranged never to see her again. I'd have had to.[6]

Love *is* love because it cannot bear to see the beloved one in pain. Love *is* love because the object of that love alone is the source of joy and gladness and pain and sorrow. *Love* is not an intransitive verb. One must love someone—or something—even if only himself or herself. Sadly, much that passes for love narcissistically claims the lover as the object of his own love. That stream of passion soon runs thin, and the end of the matter becomes a suicide of sorts. Pain will come in proportion to the love, just as joy does. As Keith grew up, my joy increased and multiplied. I watched him play Little League baseball; and my heart swelled just to see him in his ill-fitting uniform—not so much pride in his accomplishments, but *delight* in him. He played the trumpet so very well. The band concerts at school and the marching-band performances at football games were our delights. He received recognition for these things, of course. But had he not, love felt satisfied by seeing him and

knowing him in these situations. In those months of tearful to-
getherness, when we saw no performance or accomplishment,
the harmony of souls in love remained sufficient. My joy was in
him. And I needed nothing else.

God is the ultimate object of our love, for His is first and
foremost. Explain the universe apart from love—from God's
love—and you will have spoken the Great Lie, the ultimate
blasphemy. In the fragmented, splintered world of despair and
disappointment, the only eternal reference point is the unalter-
able and infinite love of God.

> Oh love of God how rich and pure how mea-
> sureless and strong
> It shall forever more endure the saints' and
> angels' song.[7]

Love is most evident in the commonplace. Love is hard-
nosed. It dwells in the everyday. Its sufficiency lies in simple
pleasures.

> Too often we search for love's lost pot of gold
> and dream of new worlds that will charm and
> excite us;
> but fantasies flee and we soon realize
> that the small things in life are the things that
> delight us.

> Simple pleasures like a baby's first tooth,
> find the treasures that you lost in your youth,
> catch a snowflake that falls on the tip of your
> tongue,

climb your ladder of dreams to the very last
  rung.

Simple pleasures like the face on a clown
catch the gold ring, ride the merry-go-round;
build a snowman and watch as it melts in the
  sun,
the moments of pain but the hours of fun.

I have two daughters, both born before Keith. To me they
were the delights of my life. They allowed me to show tenderness. Little girls, quite naturally, evoke warmth and generosity
even from insensitive men. After the day ended at the school,
where I taught, I would hurry home, plop them into the red
wagon, and pull them all over the neighborhood. The hours of
carefree enjoyment, the child's pastime, highlighted my day.
When snow fell, I'd bundle them on the sled, and we'd race
through the fleecy streets, gleefully, blissfully engaged in en-
joying God's good delights.

Love means routine and ritual without the ruts. We enjoyed
family traditions. Holidays particularly were unerringly prescribed. Keith would not allow traditions to alter. We did the
same things each Thanksgiving, each Christmas, each Easter.
Christmas held special delight. Our anticipation of Christmas
was keen, and the kids would begin preparations weeks in ad-
vance.

One ritual we unfailingly followed involved the Christmas
tree. When we moved from New Jersey to central Pennsylva-
nia, we found we could cut down our own evergreen. Each
year, about two weeks before Christmas, we would go as a
family (eventually Keith and I would go alone) and spend
hours meandering through the fields of pines and firs and blue

spruces. Our senses feasted on the cornucopia of smells and sounds there. Looking for the perfect tree, we'd stroll over the entire acreage. But the ritual, the activity itself by far held the most meaning. We'd compare the trees, but the only test a tree had to pass to be considered for selection was that it held a birds' nest. In Keith's room we assembled the collection of birds' nests gathered this way, where each new tree would have its own nest proudly displayed.

Keith would insist upon adherence to the traditions. In a throw-away world, where things change so rapidly and the treasures of the past too readily get discarded with the trash, how refreshing to find a teenager who was not beguiled by novelty. Christmas Eve's routine never deviated. The children would all sleep in Keith's room—the girls in the bunkbeds and Keith in his sleeping bag on the floor. They would whisper and giggle excitedly. I would trim the tree. That, too, was *de rigueur*. Only after they went to bed would I begin. The excitement of Christmas Day with its dazzling display of decorations, the plethora of presents under the tree, the indescribable joy, the family together.

Even now, those memories in part sustain me. In the hollow place of the heart I have stored the scenes. That rock need only be spoken to and from it flows the refreshing thoughts of tender yesterdays. Memories are magic.

What does *sonship* mean? It transcends gender! It relates relationship. On two occasions, the voice from "the excellent glory" (2 Peter 1:17) announced that "This is my son, the beloved. . . ." Eternally, God the Father loved God the Son. The very nature of the Trinity testifies to the everlasting love nature of God. Relationship and fellowship reveal the intimacy between Father and Son. By relationship Keith was my child and

my son. I had sired him. He was bone of my bone and flesh of
my flesh. Humanly, my very genes had made him. He was the
closest thing on this earth to me. What a staggering realization!
The image of myself in my son! He was not me, that I know.
But no one, in anatomy, psychology, and personality comes
closer to me. Now no longer do I know him "after the flesh."
Death alters that relationship. But perhaps the new relationship is more wonderfully complete. Eternity alone will tell.
Still, even now, I can relate to Keith in memories—beyond
memories in spirit. The apostle Paul, although physically absent from the saints, said he was present in spirit. The spirit
transcends the sensory. Frankl sensed the awareness of his wife
and had access to her spiritually, so I can hold "mystic sweet
communion" with Keith. For as believers together, death cannot dissolve those eternal bonds.

Why does God—why has God created us the way we are—
and why has He structured human society this way? I have reflected often upon the social nature of humans and the quite
apparent need we manifest for communion and companionship. God declared that it was not good for Adam to be alone
(Genesis 2:18). God is not alone. In His "Tri-unity" He is eternal community. C. S. Lewis's realization of this character of
God helped bring him to Christ. Saying that man is created in
the image of God basically and fundamentally means that we
have the created capacity for relationships. God desired that
Adam and Eve and all other humans would relate to Him, fellowship with Him, and hold communion with Him. With none
of the animals could Adam have a relationship commensurate
with his created capacity. Only with Eve. Organically in creation humans are linked together. No biblical evidence exists
that angels share an organic relationship. They were probably

created separately. Perhaps at the same time, but separately. Mankind alone, as best we know from Scripture, shares the common thread of being in descent from Adam.

Loneliness is the greatest curse for any person. One can suffer the most horrid privation and endure it as long as he has someone with whom to share, someone who cares. But loneliness, aloneness, approaches the unbearable and greatly violates our God-likeness. Whatever hell is, in its unspeakable horror, it is a place of being alone.

God the Father took from the wounded side of His Son the Church, Christ's body. As God pierced Adam's side to provide Eve, bone of his bone, so the Son's "beloved" was "born" in the sleep of Christ's substitutionary death on Calvary. And Jesus is the Firstborn among *many* brethren. Innumerable numbers of the redeemed will people heaven. Jesus Christ, the Lord, in that space of separation from God, endured the hell of cosmic loneliness that we might never be lonely or alone.

Even as Keith had been my son after the flesh, we are sons of God by faith in Jesus Christ and with the sonship is heirship. As God's heirs we will experience our rightful realm in eternity. In the sphere of time I was privileged to be a father to Keith. In heaven, whatever that place of glory holds (and the Bible talks of it sparingly), relationships surpass in purity, intensity, and permanency anything experienced upon earth. I shall enjoy Keith eternally. Jim Elliot, the martyred missionary, relates in his diary his feelings for a friend who was serving in China. His words so poignantly express my feelings.

How great shall be our fellowship in heaven! Oh, to spend eternity with such whose spirit quickens my own—makes me throb just to read his soul's surgings. But better still to see there face-to-face the Son of God whose Spirit makes [him] the way he is. How I long for another like him—one whose "love surpasses that of woman". . . . But kindred souls are few—not many are willing to bare their souls. . . .[8]

In a very moving article, Gerald Oosterveen relates his reaction to the death of his young son, and his own heartstrings quivered:

He was our first, born before we had planned to have children. I remember the pride I felt when he came, pride because he was a new generation destined to carry on our family name, pride too because he was such a beautiful and healthy child. . . . When he was not even six, the cancer came, first as foreboding suspicion, then as crushing certainty and almost always with the sharp pain that swept into oblivion the good years already past. . . . But my grief was overwhelming. . . . Perhaps I have been weeping: perhaps it is the cold, but my face is wet. I look at the stone again. "At home with Jesus," it reads and so I believe it to be. But I still miss him. I try to imagine what heaven is like. Do people there remember us, I wonder, or miss us? Some day, I reflect, I must die and will see my son again. . . . Suddenly, I felt proud to have been even if for such a short time father of this remarkable child. . . .[9]

One evening as the sky turned pewter dark and the rain fell harshly, Keith took his beloved trumpet to his lips and tried to play it. Soft tears began to roll down his cheeks. "Dad, I can't play anymore. I can't play my trumpet," he sobbed.

Keith had begun taking lessons on the trumpet in fifth grade. We had gotten him a secondhand horn on a lease program through the school, to see if he would stay with it. For seven serious years, Keith gained skill in playing, and he began an unending love affair with that instrument. On a number of occasions, he could have been discouraged, but he stayed faithfully with it. One instructor in elementary school tried to persuade him to take up the trombone or French horn, which he felt would be more suitable. Keith resisted and practiced unrelentingly. He took private lessons, and without any provoking from us, he would discipline himself and practice several hours a day. He played in the school orchestra and in the band, and one of his personal triumphs was making the high school marching band during his first year, in ninth grade, when only a handful of ninth graders successfully did so. The trumpet and music were the creative outlets of his life. During summers and the school year he worked at delivering newspapers and at other odd jobs and saved enough money to buy a silver trumpet. It was his joy. Like the bottle of the genie, he polished it every day and treated it as his prized possession. Keith took part in one of his last public performances as member of a brass ensemble that played on Easter Sunday at a local church. In that ensemble was a trumpet player of local renown whom Keith had always admired, and now he was privileged, at the age of fifteen, to play in the same group.

Keith would never again play the trumpet. He polished the horn and put it away in its case, where it remains. That night Keith and I went for a ride. I drove several hours around the area as he talked. The tears streamed down my face, and at times, I could not tell whether the rain on the windshield or tears in my eyes obscured my vision. Keith reflected on his life and family that evening. He talked, sobbingly, of his affection for us all. Then he told me that when he was very young he would look at me and wonder fearfully what would happen to him and the family if I should die.

"Maybe it's better that I die first, Dad," he said. "I don't know what I would do if you died. I couldn't bear the thought of it."

Such was my son!

How difficult now to express the way I felt then. It's not that the feelings have subsided or that time has erased the trauma. That can never happen. The experience was so profoundly personal, so subjective, so soulish that it has all been assimilated into me now. I have undergone a change more dramatic than I could have ever realized. To have lost Keith is paradoxically to have lost myself and yet to have gained myself, to have cast my bread upon the waters and now to have it back, to see the kernel fall into the ground and die and to have the new life it has yielded. If my legs were amputated, would I be the same? The doctor cannot remove the organ yet demand the function. Adaptations occur, but so does a qualitative difference. The chasm created by his departure neither goes away nor permits a proxy. I reach out to others a bit more readily, I believe. I cry more readily. I suspect too readily. I watched a television program the other day and witnessed the birth of a baby. That brought tears to my eyes. Was it Keith I saw being born? However, something in me cannot accept anything other than Keith. The love needs only him, unless it leaps beyond him to God. Poetry is one feeble way to pay tribute.

A youth in years. Of tender age
and yet a sage
in things eternal.
Vernal
sweetness and rare innocence
in matters of the world
and now your soul's unfurled
in God's grand presence.

In human wisdom, a scholar still
but a tutor without peer
in the school of courage. Nearer
to us than life you were.
We loved you like our soul.
Our goal
was God's love together,
and our heartbeats were as one.
Our son
for less than a score of years
and now shared by heaven's throng.
Love's song
transcends time.

And the trumpet that you loved to play
(now tuned to eternity's chord)
adds to the praise,
and crescendos swell sweetly
as you join the day
in adoration to the Lord,
climaxing in eternity
what you diligently pursued in time.

The Bible
your companion in the morn,
before the day's demands intruded,
fed
your soul. You were twice born.
"Children obey your parents in the Lord,"
you underscored.
Upon your bed
in pain, you whispered His name
as you did in pleasure.

Are you missed, my son? Beyond measure.
For pain is the price of love.
But in God's glory above
we shall unite
and the treasure
of eternity will be ours. Faith will be sight
and tender
touches in deathless bodies
in that splendor.

5

The Frozen Center
of My Desert Day

You think that we who do not shout and shake
Our fists at God when youth or bravery die
Have colder blood or hearts less apt to ache
Than yours who rail. I know you do. Yet why?
You have what sorrow always longs to find,
Someone to blame, some enemy in chief;
Anger's the anaesthetic of the mind,
It does men good, it fumes away their grief. . . .

So much of us, I mean, as may be left
After the dreadful process has unrolled
For one bereavement makes us more bereft.
It asks for all we have, to the last shred. . . .

Down to the frozen centre, up the vast
Mountain of pain, from world to world, he
    passed.[1]

Every pilgrim road to Jerusalem has its bare desolate tracts. Every gathered congregation could provide scores of personal stories of days of darkness
and loneliness when life seemed drained of meaning
and strength and purpose, barren days of grief and
heartache, broken hope and Paradise lost—each
story ending with the words "That was my desert
day."[2]

✢ 5 ✢

How can a person react to stressful situations, to times of disillusionment? How is a believer—a Christian, supposed to react? Is a simple, "God's will be done," enough? With a sort of benign indifference should we chalk all such circumstances up to the sovereignty of God and with stoic resignation muddle through, struggling against the pain?

It seems to me that far too frequently this has been the glib response. Who are we to take issue with God's will? Certainly, God knows what's best and whatever comes from His hand is a "good and perfect gift." Invariably Christians quote Romans 8:28 as a panacea for all ills. Anything less than resignation and docile acquiescence many interpret as rebellion against God and consider such reactions a sure indication of a lack of spirituality. Only believe! I've been told that. But can a person *only* believe? And is that a simple thing to do? How can I believe when the reality seems to contradict all that I know to be good and decent. For me no *humanly* plausible and acceptable answer exists for the horrendous death of my son. How can cancer be ordered by God? In such a time belief does not come easily. Disbelief stares at me. Naked disbelief. Lewis Smede, in his successful and refreshingly candid book, looks at the question squarely and says:

> Believing does not come easy for me either. It never has come easy; I suppose it never will. I almost always believe in God in spite of problems and pains that tell me things are so wrong that believing in a good God does not make sense. The things I say here are filtered through many years of believing against the grain. Too many people I care about hurt too much to let believing come easy. People close to me get cancer and die too soon; my prayers do not take away pain or hold back the tolling of the bells. My friends' marriages turn into battlefields and their children go through a hundred kinds of mini-hells. God does not do many miracles for my crowd.[3]

In the course of several weeks, several people I knew were diagnosed as having cancer. Since then, a number have died painful, agonizing deaths. I have known children killed in automobile accidents—promising young lives snuffed out in the springtime of youth. I hear of middle-aged people in the prime of productivity and at the peak of their capacities immobilized by disease or dead prematurely through heart failure or cancer. A middle-aged athlete in peak condition, who conscientiously cared for his body, exercising regularly, collapsed while jogging and died before anyone could reach him. A twenty-five-year-old father lies in bed while his life ebbs away, another one of cancer's victims.

I think back with great sadness to college years. A close friend, nineteen years of age, about to return to college for his junior year, with life and all its potential blossoming before him, killed in a freak automobile accident. I cried then. I questioned. Why? The inexplicable *whys!* He who had all of the virtues of youth—wholesome, sociable, athletic, godly—cut down freakishly before his life had reached fullness. An absolutely unnecessary loss—as close as one can Christianly call tragedy. Had he lived, the world would have been better for his presence. The world was a better place for the presence of my own son in it, too.

One day in 1956 I sat in the college library. How long ago it seems! But even now the scene remains vividly etched on my consciousness. I reached for the newspaper in the rack: the *Philadelphia Inquirer.* On the front page, the story was told: young missionaries savagely murdered by Indians in Latin America. Their bodies lay sprawling on the beaches in Ecuador. Young, talented men who had committed themselves uncompromisingly to Christ were now numbered among the lifeless. Almost three decades later, with hindsight's vision, we see the fruits that have come from the seeds that fell into the ground, in Ecuador, and died. But why? Must it have happened so? For wives and families pain remained. How the Christian world could have profited from those godly lives and leadership!

I see aged bodies languish in nursing homes. The minds attached to them have long since ceased to be rational. Vegetating. Serving no useful purpose. Why do *they* live? Why do we see the young so soon struck down and the weak and infirm, some of whom cry for death, hang on? Is it unchristian to ask these questions? Do such queries betray a lack of faith?

Such faith (if it be that) is the luxury of those few who have not witnessed the perversity of life's lot—the irreconcilable tension between belief that a benign Providence orders all things according to His good pleasure and the stark injustice that plagues human existence.

Did I believe Keith would be healed? Did I have any faith at all that God would raise him up? If faith was the *only* condition for Keith's healing, then Keith would live today. That kind of faith I had! I believed in God's power with unqualified certainty. I knew God could heal. Speak the word! I knew that Jesus, had He been physically present in our town, would have healed Keith. As He had raised Lazarus from the grave, He would have restored Keith to health. He would *not* have passed that need by. I remained unequivocally certain of that. So many people (well-intentioned, I'm sure) advised me that it was not—that it was *never*—God's will that people die from disease. I watched the television programs and listened to the personalities who reinforced that notion. Cancer is of the devil, they would say. God wants to give us deliverance from cancer. Claim the victory, they declared. I listened to them, and I looked at Keith. How does one reconcile these claims? Those extravagant promises for which they contend there was scriptural support! How could Keith have died of cancer if it is never God's will that His people die from cancer? Do not tell me I lack that kind of faith! I will not—I cannot believe that! At times I went past feeling, became numb beyond knowing. I felt encased in ice. With Jim Elliot, I could say:

> My love is faint; my warmth practically nil. Thoughts of His coming flicker and make me tremble. Oh, that I were not so empty-handed. Joy and

peace can come only in believing, and that is all I can say to Him tonight—Lord, I believe. I don't love; I don't feel; I don't understand; I can *only be-lieve*.[4]

As James Proctor's hymn "In Jesus" says succinctly:

> My soul is night, my heart is steel
> I cannot see, I cannot feel:
> For light, for life I must appeal
> in simple faith to Jesus.

I knew at this level, at least, I believed. And if anyone says that my belief was not belief but only presumption—that I was deceived, then I am equally deceived about everything else that I say I believe, *including* the belief that is the basis for my salvation. Do I sound angry? *I am!* I am because I've been told of this so many times. I have been told by the "celebrity world" of Christians who have high status and high visibility. Then I find it isn't true! That it is a fraud. God does not come in at the last minute to miraculously rescue the incurably ill. They die when we don't want them to. We want them to live and remain with us. Mary and Martha wept because Lazarus died. Why did they not rejoice and, when Jesus arrived in Bethany, say to Him: "Oh, Master what great joy we have. Our brother is now with God. He is in heaven where You were." But they didn't! They wept, and often in those four days after burial, they went to the grave to weep.

As Dorcas lay dead, why did not the saints sing joyfully together? When Peter came to town, they sent for him, and Peter raised her to life. Why did they not leave her in death's sleep? Could no others carry on work for the widows?

Of course, I realize I am dealing in a realm where philosophers have speculated interminably. These are not simple questions, and the answers, if they exist, are not simple. This is the purview of the perennial probing questions dealing with the ultimates and with cosmic queries. Does this puny speck, this flea, dare tangle in such turmoil? But if "faith" has *substance* (as Hebrews 11 indicates), then our belief needs a gritty, abrasive quality, for believing in a vacuum requires no faith at all, and the silky smoothness of an anaesthetized soul counts for nothing in the coarse world of contradictions.

Nature itself reveals little in its practices that permits a reverence for "Providence." C. S. Lewis confessed that appeals to nature's design or beauties provided no incentive for faith in God. On the contrary, he declared that what he witnessed testified to pain as the only enduring permanence. Nature is "red in tooth and claw" as the adage tells us. In this world of variation and flux, we can rely on the constant of pain in our lives. Interestingly, this led Lewis to formulate the fundamental dilemma: "If the universe is so bad, or even half so bad, how on earth did human beings ever come to attribute it to the activity of a wise and good Creator?"[5] How indeed?

Every time I think I have stumbled upon an answer to the problem of pain, I find myself confronted with the more perplexing questions. For me the inescapable question concerned the death of my son. Why him? Someone foolishly suggested that God was sparing my son the suffering that he would encounter in adult life. Would it not be better, this one said, to have your son spared the wickedness and evils he will inevitably meet if he lives? Folly! If that were an explanation worth considering (and it patently is not!) then, I would ask, why was he born at all? And if sixteen years of life during which I enjoyed him brought good, would not more years yield more good? Every question and answer takes us back, *reductio ad absurdum,* to prior questions that are unanswerable in finite terms. The answer is locked away in the safety of God's eternal plan. Questions become concatenated—strung out like beads, each one in turn having its antecedent but none having in itself a solution to the puzzle. The string that holds them together provides the "clue," even as Ariadne's thread led Theseus through the labyrinth to escape the minotaur. Life often becomes like a labyrinth filled with bends and blinds—a maze of the mind—and what seems to be the secret—the key to unlock the door—simply leads to another corridor and another riddle.

Our local paper heralded the exploits of a young man who risked his life to save a Lancaster County Amish girl. He had dived into the surf at the New Jersey beach and heroically had saved her. Several weeks later, he himself was killed freakishly in a motorcycle accident. Does not heroism bring with it some sort of immunity from tragedy? Reciprocity demands, doesn't it, that people who give themselves sacrificially should be saved from similar peril? But of course we know it doesn't work that way. If virtue is its own reward, my son would have been preserved from the ravages of cancer. Such a conscientious, uncomplaining, virtuous young man, in a world of the immoral, indecent, and tawdry, remained pure and unsullied. Joe Bayly, in one of his articles, told how outraged he felt when his eighteen-year-old son was killed in a sledding accident. Hit by a car and killed. His son was a moral, exemplary young man—a very rare kind of a person in a permissive, indulgent society. Bayly told how he wanted to scream against the unfairness of it all. His outrage was justified. For a youth, it surely seems correct "to rage against it."

The superficial responses so glibly given by some Christians do not suffice when so much is at stake. We cheapen grace by linking it to shoddy notions of simple assent. Dietrich Bonhoeffer rightly asked the penetrating questions as he struggled against the immense impropriety of evil in his world of the Nazi nightmare. In prison, faith could not be a simple assent— a generous benediction pronounced unctuously by the purveyors of clichés and slogans. Bonhoeffer questioned much and rightly believed in the midst of those questions. The circumstances of life are never "to be under" or "to be above," but they are "to be *through*" and only the one who has gone right through them is entitled to ask the alarming questions that seem to verge on unbelief. So Job, lying on his dung heap, scarred without and within, asks the unanswerable and in the same breath affirms that he trusts God, irrespective of what he sees and is experiencing. *Why do the righteous suffer?* Habakkuk, surveying the degradation of his times and scornfully watching the self-righteous, defiant, rebellious, hedonistic crowds of his days, asks: *Why do not the unrighteous suffer?* The lavish-living, "self-actualizers" who mock God to His face and suffer no ill! The answer comes weaving its way through the tangle: "The just shall live by Faith!" And so the just do just that. Live by faith! A faith in the face of the intolerable spectacle of innocence defiled and righteousness, amusedly, dismissed.

I am called upon by God Himself to believe that He orders everything aright. "The steps of a good man are ordered by the Lord: and he delighteth in his way" (Psalms 37:23). And so I do believe. But I *believe* in the face of the *unbelievable!* Or more precisely, I believe when my reason and logic and feelings would choose to abandon belief. I continue to *exercise* (for that's what it requires) faith in the benevolence of Almighty God when all instincts tell me not to! I persist in staking my claim to territory in the hope that I will eventually see crops grow where presently there is nothing but barrenness, or at best, brambles and briers. I believe that from the hard, defiant granite of sorrow, soon the mother lode of love will be struck, which will reveal, beneath the obstinate crust of circumstances, a tender and pure and unending rich vein of the gold of faith.

In the believing, I still grieve and have anguish. I still have within me the unfilled vacancy—the aching void of loss. It is enough for me to know he lies "safe and secure" in the arms of Jesus, but he has ceased now to be in my arms. To be a Christian does not mean living without tension. The dynamic, the "creative agonies," the seemingly irreconcilable opposites are the present realities of the Christian life. Did not the mighty apostle himself declare this:

> By honour and dishonour, by evil report and good report: as deceivers, and yet true; As unknown, and yet well known; as dying, and, behold, we live; as chastened and not killed; As sorrowful, yet always rejoicing; as poor, yet making many rich; as having nothing, and yet possessing all things.
>
> 2 Corinthians 6:8–10

Depression is a deep valley. We have all trod it at some point in our lives. Many people take only a brief journey, when the sun is obscured and shadows of sorrow darken the path for a moment. Others plod on, taking a wearisome trek through jagged ravines where no sunlight penetrates. Those months during my son's illness were lived in a netherland. I groped in the thick-shadowed world of depression. The valley deepened, and the bottom seemed to collapse beneath me. Had God not held me firmly in His grasp, I would have slipped deeply into the pit of despair. I understand a bit better now why people resort to the things they do when their pain becomes unbearable. Physical pain is unquestionably difficult to tolerate, but the inner, psychic, soulish, spiritual pain becomes burdensome beyond belief. For there is no relief. Had God not graciously guarded my emotions, I would have gone mad. Whatever one's susceptibilities, they become pronounced under stress. Temptations surface with unimaginable ferocity, and how alluringly they offer themselves as anodynes. What appeal has alcohol or drugs or the other myriad addictions? The answer is simple. Anything to deaden the pain! If only for a moment! When life is without significance and the few links to meaning break, something has to hold the feeble chain together. Something has to bond the fragments so that they don't fly off randomly. An escape. Relief. Some solace for the soul's torment. This generation, I see more clearly, has opted for these things because the daily routine provides so little relief from life's drudgeries. Fantasy—delusion—sleep—they all have their appeal. *Suicide!* The unthinkable! The unutterable word! Yet suicide increases as the cause of death in this country. How attractive the option to blot out everything with one decisive act! Do Christians commit suicide? Of course! Should they? Of course not! However, anyone who knows something about the pain of a soul overwhelmed with loneliness and despair can tell in truth that the prospect has been considered—if only fleetingly.

Hear what the psalmist says:

How long wilt thou forget me, O Lord? for ever? how long wilt thou hide thy face from me? How long shall I take counsel in my soul, having sorrow in my heart daily? How long . . . ?

Psalms 13:1, 2

In the day of my trouble I sought the Lord: my sore ran in the night, and ceased not: my soul refused to be comforted. . . . I complained, and my spirit was overwhelmed.

Psalms 77:2, 3

Hear my prayer, O Lord, and let my cry come unto thee. Hide not thy face from me in the day when I am in trouble. . . . For my days are consumed like smoke, and my bones are burned as an hearth. My heart is smitten and withered like grass; so that I forget to eat my bread. By reason of the voice of my groaning my bones cleave to my skin. I am like a pelican of the wilderness: I am like an owl of the desert. I watch, and am as a sparrow alone upon the house top. . . . For I have eaten ashes like bread, and mingled my drink with weeping. . . . My days are like a shadow that declineth; and I am withered like grass.

Psalms 102:1–7, 9, 11

And listen to the words of the prophet and the patriarch:

But he himself went a day's journey into the wilderness, and came and sat down under a juniper tree: and he requested for himself that he might die; and

113

said, It is enough; now, O Lord, take away my life; for I am not better than my fathers.

1 Kings 19:4

And Job spake, and said, Let the day perish wherein I was born, and the night in which it was said, There is a man child conceived. Let that day be darkness; let not God regard it from above, neither let the light shine upon it. Let darkness and the shadow of death stain it; let a cloud dwell upon it; let the blackness of the day terrify it. As for the night, let darkness seize upon it; let it not be joined unto the days of the year, let it not come into the number of the months. Lo, let that night be solitary, let no joyful voice come therein. . . . Why died I not from the womb? why did I not give up the ghost when I came out of the belly? . . . For now should I have lain still and been quiet, I should have slept: then had I been at rest. . . . Wherefore is light given to him that is in misery, and life unto the bitter in soul; Which long for death but it cometh not; and dig for it more than for hid treasures; Which rejoice exceedingly, and are glad, when they can find the grave? . . . I was not in safety, neither had I rest, neither was I quiet; yet trouble came.

Job 3:2–7, 11, 13, 20–22, 26

John Paton lived during the last century. He left a comfortable life in Scotland and, in response to Christ's command, spent his life in service for the gospel in foreign lands, including the cannibal-infested New Hebrides. Within a short time after his arrival in that primitive part of the world, and soon after he undertook his ministry, both his young wife and baby died. Years later, he recorded his response in his autobiography.

> Stunned by that dreadful loss, in entering upon this field of labor to which the Lord had Himself so evidently led me, my reason seemed for a time almost to give way. Ague and fever, too, laid a depressing and weakening hand upon me, continuously recurring and reaching oftentimes the very height of its worst burning stages. But I was never altogether forsaken. The ever-merciful Lord sustained me, to lay the precious dust of my beloved Ones in the same quiet grave, dug for them close by my own hands, despite breaking heart, had to take the principal share. I built the grave round and round with coral blocks, and covered the top with beautiful white coral, broken small as gravel; and that spot became my sacred and much-frequented shrine, during all the following months and years when I labored on for the salvation of these savage Islanders amidst the difficulties, dangers and deaths. Whensoever Tanna turns to the Lord and is won for Christ, men in after-days will find the memory of that spot still green—where with ceaseless prayers and tears I claimed that land for God in which I had "buried my dead" with faith and hope. But for Jesus and the fellowship he vouchsafed me there I must have gone mad and died beside that lonely grave.[6]

Gone mad! How many, if they are honest, will confess that they, in circumstances like Paton's, have welcomed that pros-

pect. When life's foundations seem to crumble into dust—
when the fires of adversity burn up everything that we hold
dear—do we not wish secretly for another world? Does God
take from us the very dear things—the very dear ones—so that
heaven becomes the place of our affection, so that we will
"seek those things that are above. . ."? Not a day passes when
my thoughts do not fly skyward to that place Christ is preparing. While waiting for "that blessed hope" I wonder if this frail
flame will continue to flicker in faithfulness to Him.

> Yet I am frail, O Lord. Frail as dust.
> Not delicate
> Like the leaf
> or the diaphanous wings of the butterfly
> or the silky thread of the worm,
> but frail.
> Ready, O God, to dissolve at the touch.
>
> As though the sunlight fell on parchment,
> centuries old,
> hidden in musty archives
> and disintegrated it.
> I am without strength.
>
> My visions fill the landscape
> stretching endlessly beyond horizons.
> Outward
> Upward
> spiraling like the smoke
> then dissipate
> lost in foggy mists that are washed away
> by rains of time.
> Great my aspirations. Weak my capacities.

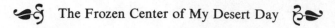

If I long to be sticks lit by divine fire
to burn (as Saint Elliot prayed)
I find the faggots are tender and green
and will not ignite.
Seasoned wood burns better. Of aged timbers
conflagrations come.
The consumption of the soul's fuel
on which the Spirit feeds.

Am I too frail, O Lord?

As frail as fire!

6

Fellowship
of His Suffering

Love's as warm as tears.
  Love is tears:
Pressure within the brain,
Tension at the throat. . . .

Love's as fierce as fire.
  Love is fire:
All sorts—infernal heat. . . .

Love's as fresh as spring.
  Love is spring:
Bird-song hung in the air,
Cool smells in a wood,
Whispering 'Dare! Dare!'

119

Love's as hard as nails,
  Love is nails:
Blunt, thick, hammered through
The medial nerves of One
Who, having made us, knew
The thing He had done,
Seeing (with all that is)
Our cross, and His.[1]

⤝ 6 ⤟

We have no intimate knowledge of God apart from suffering. The apostle Paul desired, "That I may know him ... and the fellowship of his sufferings ..." (Philippians 3:10). A long time ago, somewhere along the way in my Christian experience, this verse was given to me. It became my life's verse. I can't recall the circumstances that confirmed that conviction, but I know it to be true. I had longed to have that full, experiential knowledge of Christ (Greek: *epignosis*) about which Paul passionately spoke and that he unreservedly sought.

"As the hart panteth after the water brooks, so panteth my soul after thee, O God" (Psalms 42:1). I would read these words and my "bowels of compassion" yearned to have this inner thirst for God slaked. A burning, intense desire to know Jesus Christ beyond the commonplace of mere acquaintance! The Old Testament in the quaint King James English uses the term "know" to express the most intimate of relationships—that between a man and a woman, between a husband and

wife. "Adam knew Eve. . . ." The coupling of flesh as two become one in the nuptial delights unspeakably innocent and
tender. The rapturous revelation of such knowledge is no more
exquisitely and delicately described than in the Song of Solomon. Listen to the words and phrases that weave themselves
into the timeless tapestry of *agape* love.

> Let him kiss me with the kisses of his mouth: for thy
> love is better than wine. The king hath brought me
> into his chambers: we will be glad and rejoice in
> thee, we will remember thy love more than wine.
> Tell me O thou, whom my soul loveth where thou
> feedest. Behold thou are fair my love. Behold thou
> art fair my beloved. I sat down under his shadow
> with great delight and his fruit was sweet to my
> taste. He brought me to his banqueting house, and
> his banner over me was love. His left hand is under
> my head, and his right hand doth embrace me. The
> voice of my beloved! He cometh leaping upon the
> mountains, skipping upon the hills. My beloved is
> like a roe or a young hart. My beloved spoke and
> said unto me Rise up, my love, my fair one and
> come away. Arise my love, my fair one and come
> away. O my dove, thou art in the clefts of the rock,
> in the secret places of the stairs, let me see thy coun-
> tenance, let me hear thy voice; for sweet is thy voice
> and thy countenance is lovely. By night on my bed I
> sought him whom my soul loveth. Saw ye him
> whom my soul loveth? . . . stir not up nor awake my
> love till he please. Behold thou art fair my love; be-
> hold thou art fair. Thou art fair my love; there is no
> spot in thee. Thou hast ravished my heart. . . . Thou

hast ravished my heart. . . . How fair is thy love. . . . How much better is thy love than wine! And the smell of thy ointments than all spices. Thy lips . . . drop as the honeycomb: honey and milk are under thy tongue; and the smell of thy garments like the smell of Lebanon.

Awake, O north wind; and come, thou south; blow upon my garden, that the spices thereof may flow out. Let my beloved come into his garden and eat his pleasant fruits. I sleep but my heart waketh; it is the voice of my beloved that knocketh, saying, Open to me, my sister, my love, my dove, my undefiled. My beloved put in his hand by the hole of the door and my bowels were moved for him. I rose up to open to my beloved. My beloved is white and ruddy, the chiefest among ten thousands. He is altogether lovely. This is my beloved and this is my friend.

Song of Solomon 1:2–5:16 *passim*

To have such an intimate, personal knowledge of the Lord Jesus was Paul's desire, but he could not obtain it apart from suffering. Love can never be separated from suffering. A cosmic law—a divine decree—sets suffering as the prerequisite, the precondition for the intimacy of love knowledge. To this, all true artists assent. Poet and painter alike know that the vital difference between artist and amateur, between artisan and the tinker, between devotee and the dilettante is suffering. The universal decree we cannot abrogate testifies to the transmutation of love's capacity for suffering into the eternal worth of the deed.

Nobody likes to suffer. Humans direct much activity toward

avoiding or reducing suffering. And this is as it should be. Suffering is not in itself inherently good. In fact, the proclivity of people to put themselves in circumstances that bring on suffering is pathological. In masochistic moods that foster despair we see symptoms of mental instability. However, suffering forms an inevitable part of life and necessarily is a precondition for growth and life itself. Suffering involves struggle, whether it's the fight against forces and circumstances that assail us from without or the struggle against inner tensions and conflicts. The sperm propels itself, laboring in the quest for union with the egg, which when fertilized creates life. From growth in the womb through eruption from that intrauterine state into the maze of life's demands, until death's final gasp, struggle is the inevitable lot of life.

Tiny seeds push against seemingly impenetrable crust of soil, seeking sunlight. The butterfly toils to tear away the cocoon that has protected it, but from which it now must free itself. A chick pecks away at the shell, cracking the coating, which must now be discarded. Life in its various forms struggles to survive and through the long, arduous development, finds its significance.

> There is this as well: I was always bewitched by three of God's creatures—the worm that becomes a butterfly, the flying fish that leaps out of the water in an effort to transcend its nature, and the silkworm that turns its entrails into silk. I always felt a mystical unity with them, for I always imagined them as symbols symbolizing the route of my soul. . . . For me, the grub's yearning to become a butterfly always stood as its—and man's—most imperative and at

the same time, most legitimate duty. . . . A faithful
Christian would have said to me . . . You did not see
worms, you saw us—human beings.[2]

Paul Tournier documented that "deprivation" is the critical
correlate of creativity.[3] Deprivation involves loss of someone
or something of significance. The natural assumption is that
loss leads to defeat or results in a disfigured and damaged life.
Disfigured—perhaps! But damaged—not necessarily. If we
think merely in terms of cosmetic culture, which sees defects as
disadvantages, then we conclude that anything that does not
correspond to the ideal image causes reduction in value. However, such a perspective fails to recognize that God, in this sin-
marred cosmos, uses the defect to create the more superior
work. The potter Jeremiah observed did not discard the defective clay, but reshaped it, producing a far more exquisite
craftsmanship, using as the key for the design the presumed
defect (Jeremiah 18: 3, 4). The cross of our Lord Jesus Christ
has become for all time the motif about which God has woven
the redemptive tapestry of His work of restoration.

A biographer of the British writer-critic Malcolm Muggeridge has noted that "for many people suffering is the major
stumbling block on the path to Christian faith." He likewise
noted that this was *not* the case for Muggeridge.

Muggeridge sees suffering as something basic and
integral to human life, like sharps and flats are to
music. Take away the sharps and flats and there is
no music; take away suffering, and there is no life.
. . . The contemporary man who turns his back on a
drama in which suffering is an essential part and

hearkens instead to the sedulous of the doctors and the eugenicists who promise to eliminate suffering, perhaps even death itself, is fashioning a tragedy by his own hand.[4]

Suffering is both an enigma and the most understandable occurrence in the world. We know and long for *goodness*. As humans, we abhor the suffering that occurs at every level of life. From minor, unavoidable perplexities to the vast horror of holocausts! Unless we have become desensitized to life's horrors or psychopathic in personality, we cringe at the sight of suffering. Why is such indecency permitted? Readily we would expunge the word *suffering* from our vocabularies. Paradoxically, we know, in this world of the dislocation, that suffering will not only be there, but *should* be there. It has its logical and legitimate part, and within ourselves, we sense that the only purification that can purposefully occur comes through suffering. Its fire cauterizes contamination. It, like Elisha's salt, alone can sweeten waters now acrid and unpotable.

One can no more eliminate suffering from life ... than one can eliminate suffering from *King Lear* and still have a play. . . . It is those who imagine that life can be bent to conform with their own vain hopes and aspirations and whose disillusionment when this fails, as fail it must, knows no bounds, who are the rankest pessimists. . . . Yet one can dimly see and humbly say that suffering is an integral and essential part of our human drama. That it falls upon one and all in differing degrees and forms whose comparison lies beyond competence. That it belongs to God's

purpose for us here on earth, so that in the end all
the experience of living has to teach us is to say: Thy
will be done. To say it standing before a cross; itself
signifying the suffering of God in the person of man,
and the redemption of man in the person of God.
The greatest sorrow and the greatest joy co-existing
on Golgotha.[5]

Suffering is universal and is unique. We all share together in
the ubiquitous anguish of grief. Suffering yields grief. Do we
not respond with grief to a condition in which we suffer? Voy-
agers we all are on this odyssey of outrage, assailed relentlessly
by the tempests of everyday life. None claims exemption. All
suffer. And our personal suffering, although shared, being
"such as is common to man," nevertheless remains uniquely
our own. No one carries another's grief. Share we may, but a
"stone's throw" distance invariably separates each of us from
all others in suffering. Gethsemanes seldom become gathering
places. As each of us receives the call to endure suffering we
cannot sentimentalize or trivialize it. Some types of suffering
elicit outrage. Others, seemingly less significant, at best evoke
pity. However, as Viktor Frankl has noted:

A man's suffering is similar to the behavior of gas. If
a certain quantity of gas is pumped into an empty
chamber, it will fill one chamber completely and
evenly, no matter how big the chamber. Thus suffering completely fills the human soul and conscious
mind, no matter whether the suffering is great or little. Therefore the "size" of human suffering is absolutely relative.[6]

Psalms 42 and 43 combined became for me an absorbing daily devotional. During my son's illness I remained unable to frame anything original. My prayers were, monotonously, supplications for his healing and for my own stability. The Psalter is the source of support, I found, in which Christ is most manifestly "touched with the feelings of our infirmities."

> My soul thirsteth for God, for the living God: when shall I come and appear before God? My tears have been my meat day and night. . . . I pour out my soul in me. . . . Why art thou cast down, O my soul? and why art thou disquieted in me? hope thou in God: for I shall yet praise him for the help of his countenance. O my God, my soul is cast down within me. . . . Why art thou cast down, O my soul? and why art thou disquieted within me? hope thou in God.
>
> Psalms 42:2–11 *passism*

Ten times between the two psalms the question *why* arises. True suffering will always wring from our lips, our hearts, the cry—*why?*

Suffering and tears are companions. The psalmist describes tears as his food. During the time of Keith's illness and the months that painfully followed, I shed more tears than in the preceding years. Sheldon Vanauken, in his intensely personal love story, *A Severe Mercy,* confesses that after the death of his beloved wife, Davy, "The tears came freely, and I did not attempt to refrain them when I was alone."[7]

In one of A. W. Tozer's writings, which I cannot presently recall, Tozer tells about a missionary who spoke in Tozer's church in Chicago, and during the message the missionary broke down in tears. He later told Tozer that he had recently had an experience in his life that had changed him quite remarkably, and now he found himself weeping readily. Tozer assured that man that his tears were both refreshing and indicative of a sensitive soul, for so few seemed to be able to weep anymore.

I find the tears flow freely. I read recently in a commentary on the book of Revelation that the apostle John's tearful response to the inability of anyone to open the scroll in heaven, as recorded in chapter 4 of that book, was the *only* instance of anyone crying in heaven. Thank God, the Lamb appeared who was worthy to open the scroll, and John was told to cease his weeping. This very morning as I was writing these words, reflecting on the tears that sorrow brings, I read from *Our Daily Bread* devotional:

> What a strange yet beautiful text this is! Imagine being nourished by tears! Even though there are times in life when they are our daily portion eternity will certainly reveal that we gained more strength and spiritual stature through sorrow than through either prosperity or the shallow experiences of temporary happiness. . . . May we not shun the heaven-sent sustenance, but humbly allow our sorrows to draw us closer to the Savior. By yielding to Him, our tears can become nourishment for our souls.
>
> > I walked a mile with sorrow
> > and never a word said she;
> > but oh, the things I learned from her
> > when sorrow walked with me.[8]

But the temptation is strong to assume that Christians are different. Does not God immunize us when we become His children? Does He not grant us exemption from the suffering that characterizes the world? How we would like to believe that! How glorious we think, for God to wrap us up in a mystical suffer-proof garment and for us to dance through life, oblivious to discord and sadness. But we know it is not like that and that it cannot be like that. Paul, the suffering apostle, reminded the Philippian believers that "For unto you it is given in the behalf of Christ, not only to believe on him, but also to suffer for his sake" (1:29). Suffering is our lot—may I say our *blessed* lot. The Christian life does not automatically provide the great insights into suffering. Some overwhelming sufferings neither piety nor reason settles. The realm of religion is not the place to go for quick-fix answers to soul-wrenching suffering. C. S. Lewis, who thought more deeply about these things than most people do, knew that. "Don't come talking to me about the consolations of religion or I shall suspect that you don't understand."[9]

James Stewart, with characteristic clarity, declares that "the first thing Christianity does to the problem of suffering is to heighten and accentuate the difficulty of it."[10] No simple solution exists. Beware the person who can quickly identify God's purposes in your sorrow and suffering! These "seers" abound. The glib pronouncement, reminiscent of Job's comforters, only adds to the misery.

Even if an answer were forthcoming, would it have dried my tears and mended my broken heart? Would the pain that penetrated and pulsated like a throbbing nerve have subsided? My loss was real—painfully real. Christ our Lord *knew* what was to befall Him. He knew what events would soon transpire in

His own life. The Scriptures say ". . . Jesus knew that his hour was come that he should depart out of this world. . ." (John 13:1). "Jesus knowing that all things were now accomplished . . ." (John 19:28). Our Lord knew with His own penetrating awareness the suffering that would fill His sinless life, yet He willingly chose the path that pleased the Father. The knowing did not reduce the pain. It did not minimize the suffering. Indeed, for Him, it accentuated it all.

What does it mean to suffer? Definitions are hard to come by. Suffering is at best defined in the doing, but no suffering takes place without the knowing of it. Smedes attempts this definition:

> To suffer is to put up with things you very much want not to put up with. If you badly want to be rid of something and it will not go away, you are suffering. It may be only a nuisance—a fly buzzing madly in circles, never landing anywhere in your bedroom, when you are wild for want of sleep. It may be a guilt whose sting you feel until you die— the memory of having betrayed a spouse. Suffering can be a physical pain like a headache or bone cancer. It can be mental anguish, like the desperate loneliness that sets in when a loved one dies. . . . Suffering . . . then is a feeling that things are wrong with us and we cannot make them right.[11]

Anyone who has suffered knows this. "When a loved one dies. . . ." The intensity of that suffering was in "fellowship with Christ." I have never known any degree of pain like that which split my soul open and laid its vital nerve bare. In this winepress the stones did grind me into dust—the dust of death as the psalmist put it. Never did I experience that before, and that has been the closest I have come to sharing in the sufferings of the Savior. It is a *given* in the Christian life, Paul says, that we suffer. If we share the suffering, we share the glory. The nature of the circumstances are different for each of us and distinctive to us. God in wisdom and benevolence suits the suffering to the needs of our lives, to the task He must accomplish. God's ways surely are not our ways.

I find myself seeking ready resolution to the ambiguity that clutters my life. My childish penchant for vivid, clear dichotomies remains. However, I find that God does not conform Himself to clean character lines. I want the consequences clearly related to the condition. Let's have firm, fixed linkages. I seek cleanness—sharp, defined focus. Fuzzy images that fade in and out bother me. If I am suffering, I want to know that God has tied that to some identifiable growth process. I need, in other words, to gauge the glory according to the trial. It just doesn't happen. Peter identifies the unmistakable relationship between suffering and glory but he tells us that we "suffer a while" and afterward the glory will come (1 Peter 5:10).

Smedes describes suffering as a gift. Curious! Yet I suppose he is right. Some sufferings cannot be avoided, and we have no choice in the matter. There we have only the choice about our *attitude* toward the suffering. Again, Frankl has told us:

> ... Everything can be taken from a man but one thing: the last of the human freedoms—to choose one's attitude in any given set of circumstances to choose one's way.... Fundamentally, therefore, any man can, under such circumstances, decide what

132

shall become of him—mentally and spiritually. There is only one thing that I dread: not to be worthy of my suffering.[12]

But there are times when we can choose to suffer or not to suffer. Moses chose a course of suffering when the alternative was open to him. "By faith Moses, when he was come to years, refused to be called the son of Pharaoh's daughter; Choosing rather to suffer affliction with the people of God, than to enjoy the pleasures of sin for a season" (Hebrews 11: 24, 25). We find the key to this decision in the phrase, "when he was come to years." When we are mature in His purposes, God will give to us a similar choice. As long as we remain infantile and untested, the suffering that He calls upon us to endure is principally the unavoidable kind. In such situations attitude will determine the profit we may accrue from that experience. But as we mature we begin to face critical times—the crisis, the crux, the cross—when we *choose* to suffer or not to suffer. The choice was transparent for Moses. It would have taken no effort to remain in the comfort of Egyptian luxury and the opulence of painlessness it afforded. The choice was an *active* one. He must decide to cast his lot with God's people and risk everything. The consequences of such a choice for that man meant, decisively, deprivation.

Smedes contrasts suffering *for* and suffering *with*. I can choose my suffering *with* as freely as Moses chose his suffering *with* the people of God. I *chose* to suffer *with* my son, Keith. The immediate choice was, of course, preceded by a lengthy chain of choices all linked together by love. He was my child, and the natural parental bond connected us. However, plenty of parents quite callously disregard their offspring without any tinge of guilt. Tales of this type of treatment horrify us daily. Keith was my *only* son. The father-son relationship link strengthens the bond. However, some fathers care little for their own sons. With regret I recall my own father's indifference toward his sons. He could not distinguish among us years later. During our childhood, he showed little concern.

I would have chosen no other option than to suffer with Keith, if other options had been available. I stayed with him day after day. The agonizing hours and days that we both knew would lead toward a separation became times of intensely shared suffering. Keith suffered outrageously. Physical pain intensifying daily—the cancer consuming his organs and constricting bowels and bladder—the nausea and vomiting episodes convulsing his entire body. The emotional agony of a life ebbing away. A young man who now faced his own imminent death! Keith would sit during the night, depressed and frightened, telling me he didn't want to die. "Why can't things be as they were before?" he would sigh despairingly. He wanted to be with his friends. He was restricted, at first to the house, then to his room, and then to the bed. He could not eat regularly. The excruciating pain overwhelmed him. I sat by him and with him, suffering as I had never done before.

> Let's have no foolishness about suffering being nice after all because it makes us saints. We are talking about real suffering, and suffering is not liking what you've got. But the power of love gives a person energy to choose it anyway, simply to share it with the person who is stuck with it. You choose it and you stick with it, you twist and turn, you hang by your finger nails, you wish to God it would go away but

you choose to feel it as long as the other person feels it. That is what love does to you. . . . while he is slowly, surely, devoured by cancer.[13]

Keith's suffering was a cold, bare fact. No one could tone it down. Sharp, daggerlike needles injected into his frail body, filled with morphine or Demerol, dramatized the irony of the ordeal. Pain to deal with pain. I cannot recall ever being so involved with a sufferer. My own experiences in life pale into insignificance when I compare them to my son's. Now—at this very moment—it remains difficult to find the words, the proper expressions that capture the reality of the experience. The only thing that I can relate as a parallel is the suffering of the Savior. My son's sufferings approximated those of the Lord Jesus. In Keith's illness, God provided me with a parable of the travail of His Son. The comparisons became vivid. I saw the dying agony of Christ miniaturized in Keith.[14]

The startling aspect of suffering is that it is a vital part (*the* vital part!) of God's redemptive plan. In the grand cosmic scheme that God in infinite wisdom and infinite love has designed, suffering forms the cornerstone of the eternal edifice. When we seek to understand the reasons of the origin of sin in the world and in the universe we can only speculate. The imponderables that lead us back into the eternal recesses of God's counsels allow us to conclude that God is working "according to the eternal purpose which he purposed in Christ Jesus our Lord" (Ephesians 3:11). Why Lucifer fell—why Satan was allowed access to Adam and Eve—why God permitted the chain of events that have plunged this globe into chaos and despair—these questions have their answers only in the unchanging nature of the very being of God, whom we are told is

Love. Therefore, we inevitably conclude that suffering is an inextricable element of love. The pointed needle of pain is necessary in the weaving of the cosmic tapestry that God will in that glorious day reveal to the universe.

Ernest Gordon, who suffered severely under the Japanese in a World War II POW camp on the infamous Kwai River, describes his own understanding of life in similar terms.

> I recalled that when I was at Paisley I had been told how the old-time weavers, all the while they were making their beautiful and intricate patterns, saw no more than the backs of their shawls. Nothing was visible to them but a tangle of colored threads. They never saw the design they were creating until they took the finished fabric from their looms.
> The parallel to the mortal lot is plain. Human experience appears to us—as the shawls did to the weavers—to be no more than incomprehensible tangles of colored threads, whereas in fact life represents the ordered threads in a great design—the design being woven daily on the loom of eternity. Looking back, in all the chaos and confusion, I could see a splendid purpose being worked out.[15]

The banner of the suffering saints of God is spangled with stars who will shine in the firmament of God's Day. Doubtless many remain at this point obscure and unheralded. Like Keith, they have suffered isolation and anonymity. Some in hospital and care facilities. Others in prisons and internment camps. The nature of the suffering and the circumstances are of less importance than the purposes for the suffering and the re-

sponse to it. Do we suffer courageously? Do we uncomplain-
ingly endure pain as those who commit their souls to God?

From the many horror stories that have surfaced from the
Nazi holocaust, the heroic stories of God's people who ac-
cepted the bestial behavior from their fellow humans as from
the hands of the gracious God stand out sharply. Dietrich
Bonhoeffer, a German pastor, exemplifies the resolution to be
faithful unto death. Bonhoeffer was executed by orders of
Himmler in 1945. Of suffering, Bonhoeffer says this:

> Each must endure his allotted share of suffering and
> rejection. But each has a different share: some God
> deems worthy of the highest form of suffering, and
> gives them the grace of martyrdom. . . . Suffering,
> then, is the badge of true discipleship. The disciple is
> not above his master. Following Christ means *passio
> passiva,* suffering because we have to suffer. . . . Dis-
> cipleship means allegiance to the suffering Christ,
> and it is therefore not at all surprising that Chris-
> tians should be called upon to suffer. . . . Suffering
> means being cut off from God, yet within the fel-
> lowship of Christ's sufferings, suffering is overcome
> by suffering, and becomes the way to communion
> with God. Suffering has to be endured that it might
> pass away.[16]

How different this attitude is from the prevailing prescrip-
tion of the Christian life. Panaceas proliferate, and we typically
associate the marks of commitment to Christ with the standards of success that this world values. Material prosperity,

power, privilege, position, freedom from pain, invincibility—these we view as signs of God's commendation. The wise words of Stewart refute this naive and erroneous notion: "In the making of the soul, and in the producing of life's deepest and profoundest harmony, suffering has a positive and creative function to fulfil."[17]

We are God's workmanship, crafted along lines of most exquisite and tender care. We are God's "poetry" (Ephesians 2:10; Greek: *poiema*), and He often uses a discordant meter; nevertheless, the completed composition is always a masterpiece.

> It is. . . . the power of sorrow and trouble to chisel the spirit and beautify the character and deepen the whole life.[18]

> But page after page there would be to tell how trouble and difficulty and bereavement and bitter disappointment and hopes frustrated and dreams that flickered out and died—all the things which hurt and leave a mark—had brought blessing by imparting new depth, new insight to the soul.[19]

> Every soul that takes its personal griefs and troubles and offers these up on the altar alongside the sacrifice of Jesus is sharing constructively in that eternal passion of God by which all humanity shall at last find healing and peace.[20]

God used the writings of many saints to strengthen me during the siege of suffering. What strength I found in the words of others who have, too, been tried in the furnace! I confess that I have little time for the superficialities that pass for today's wisdom. The much too quickly written lyric of the Christian song fails to comfort or console. In times of spiritual thirst, when trials intensify, nothing less than buckets of spiritual water, drawn from deep wells, will suffice. We find the saints in Scripture (Moses, Abraham, Isaac, David, and so on) and Christ Himself sitting upon wells. Abraham dug his well at Beersheba and "called there on the name of the Lord, the everlasting God" (Genesis 21:33). Isaac, the emulator, dug only those wells which his father Abraham had dug and he ". . . called their names after the names by which his father had called them" (Genesis 26:18). Moses fled from Egypt, and in the land of Midian, ". . . he sat down by a well" (Exodus 2:15). David, exiled from his boyhood home at Bethlehem, desired to drink from the well he had known since his childhood. "Oh that one would give me drink of the water of the well of Bethlehem, which is by the gate!" (2 Samuel 23:15). The very first reference in Scripture to a watering hole involved Hagar's hasty departure from Abraham's household. God met her at "a fountain of water in the wilderness." There He made Hagar aware of "him that seeth me" (Genesis 16:13).

The classic hymn of Annie Cousins, based on the writings of Samuel Rutherford, so well expresses the source of strength:

> O Christ, He is the fountain,
> The deep sweet, well of love!
> The streams on earth I've tasted
> More deep I'll drink above:
> There to an ocean fulness
> His mercy doth expand,
> And glory, glory dwelleth
> In Immanuel's land.

In the *Letters of Samuel Rutherford,* God provided for me daily delights. From a man who lived more than three centuries ago, I was refreshed. Rutherford had lost his wife after she had endured a lengthy illness, and then both of his children had died. The compiler of his letters has written: "Such was the discipline by which he was trained for the duties of a pastor, and by which a shepherd's heart of true sympathy was imparted to him."[21]

Writing to Lady Kenmure, with whom he had frequent correspondence, Rutherford knew that she also had lost several children, and he reminds her:

> ... Your part in this case (seeing God taketh nothing from you but that which he is to supply with his own presence), to desire your Lord to know his own room and take it even upon Him to come in, in the room of dead children.[22]

To a friend, Marion McNaught, he wrote in 1635:

> ... We poor children, far from home, must steal through many waters, weeping as we go and withal believing that we do the Lord's faithfulness no wrong.[23]

Again writing to Lady Kenmure:

> ...Now in your solitary life when your comforts outward are few ... I know his love to you is still running over, and his love hath not so bad a memory as to forget you and your dear child, who hath

two fathers in heaven, the one the Ancient of Days.[24]

To Alexander Gordon of Earlston, he gave this comfort:

Thank God that Christ came to your house in your absence and took with him some of your children. He presumed that much on your love that ye would not offend. ... If ye were not Christ's wheat, appointed to be bread in his house, he would not grind you.[25]

Sunday, the Lord's Day, the early morning hours followed a trying evening. Keith slept little during the night, because of the severe pain. I had given him an injection, which had little effect, so I called the attending physician, who prescribed morphine, to be taken orally. Never before had I given Keith morphine, and I associated it with the end of things. I had dreaded the day when I would have to remove the bottle from the shelf and let him sip spoonfuls of the unpleasant liquid. Fiery fingers electrified my mind with fear as I unscrewed the cap from that loathsome bottle. On this morning, the first of many, the fright of death's imminency overtook me. From Rutherford's letters, I read these words, written to Robert Gordon in 1637:

All that I dow [am able to do] is to hold out a lame faith to Christ, like a beggar holding out a stump, instead of an arm or leg, and cry, "Lord Jesus, work a miracle." Oh, what would I give to have hands and arms to grip strongly and fold heartsomely about

Christ's neck, and to have my claim made good with real possession.[26]

Later, in the wearisome days that followed, the deterioration accelerated and the pain became more pronounced, and tears and prayers filled my nights. I slept fitfully if I slept at all. My son's world, increasingly restricted, centered on pain, now the pulse center of his life.

A year ago, I would reflect, life was blissfully routine. Only minor vexations intruded upon my world. The sense of firm faith and the giddiness that often go with sweet indifference to trials had been my sweet luxuries. Now, a year later, time became tedious and fractures and fissures widened in my plastered faith.

> We can in our prosperity, sport ourselves and be too bold with Christ; yea, be that insolent as to chide with Him; but under the water we dare not speak. I wonder now of my sometime boldness to chide and quarrel Christ, to nickname Providence when it stroked me against the hair; for now swimming in the waters, I think my will is fallen to the ground of the water; I have lost it.[27]

The summer wore on and wore me down. Daily, I felt the bathyspheric weight of the waters of the suffering of my soul. I saw Keith slipping beyond me. Do not expect him to live longer than two months, the doctors had told us, and soon the two months would terminate. Could I let him go? Could I now let God take the very one whom I had given? It is one thing for Abraham to see the host of heaven and believe God. It is not difficult to let the sand sift through his fingers and know that his seed will be similarly prodigious. But *one* son—a *solitary,* beloved son now on the altar of sacrifice! Can faith survive this?

> Let your children be as so many flowers borrowed from God: if the flower die or wither, thank God for a summer loan of them and keep good neighborhood, to borrow and lend with Him. Set your heart upon heaven and trouble not your spirit with this clay-idol of the world, which is but vanity and hath but the luster of the rainbow in the air, which cometh and goeth with a flying March-shower.[28]

I confess that on more than one occasion I sought to find indications that God would heal my son. Various references occurred in my daily meditations, from which I felt tempted to take signs that God would raise him up. I hoped God was vouchsafing these to me as true indicators of His intent to work the miracle.

> But will I not believe that God will take this advantage of me, when my back is at the wall. He who forbiddeth to add affliction to affliction, will He do it Himself.[29]

> I know His comforts are no dreams; He would not put his Seal on blank paper, nor deceive His afflicted ones that trust in Him.[30]

> But Christ's love is neither a cruel nor unkind mercy, but the love-token of a father.[31]

In the sultry heat of July, I wrote in the margin of the reading: "After a night of heaviness and sorrow, may, O Lord, this be true for Keith." The reading that day in Rutherford's letters concerned a friend, John Kennedy, who set sail to greet his friend, whose small vessel appeared to be swallowed up in the waves. Kennedy's friend, upon learning of this, secluded himself for three days. He then went to visit Kennedy's wife "under her supposed bereavement." At that very time, Kennedy made his appearance, to the great joy of all. I forced an interpretation that God would do this for Keith and me. It turned out not to be true.

> Yet I am in this hot summer-blink with the tear in my eye; for (by reason of my silence) sorrow, sorrow hath filled me; my harp is hanged upon the willow trees. . . .[32]
> Hold on! Christ never yet slew a sighing, groaning child. . . .[33]

Five days after I read this, Keith died. My soul was in inexpressible anguish. These words came from Rutherford: "No loss is comparable to the loss of a soul; there is no hope of regaining that loss."[34]

Consolation lay in knowing that Keith knew the Lord Jesus. He knew the Friend of the helpless and weak and the fragile. In his youth, Keith had committed himself in gentle trust to the Savior.

> Desire your children in the morning of their life, to begin and seek the Lord and to remember the Creator in the days of their youth. . . . Let the Lord have the flower of their age; the best sacrifice is due Him.

> Instruct them in this, that they have a soul in them
> to fear the name of the great and dreadful God, who
> hath laid up great things for those that love and fear
> Him! I pray that God may be their portion.[35]

God will not allow the limited perspective of time to cloud His grand vision of eternity. His people often too willingly settle for the immediate, ephemeral hours of happiness, when the unending "pleasures at his right hand" await. "And it may be that God counts a human life of seventy years of suffering not too long an education for a soul which may serve Him through the eternities."[36] We dare not let "our light affliction which is but for a moment" obscure the "far more exceeding and eternal weight of glory" (2 Corinthians 4:17). Suffering is the "signal of transcendence" that points us beyond the present world and tells us to keep eternity clearly in view. Without suffering, we would too quickly become engulfed with "the cares of this world and the deceitfulness of riches" and would contentedly "tether our tents." The pilgrim character of our lives would be abandoned; our tents, intended to be pitched and temporary, would soon become securely permanent; and the Father's house of "many mansions" would lose its appeal.

Suffering becomes a ministry. It performs a peculiar alchemy that transforms harshness and intemperance into tenderness. The suffering heart melts like the icy waters of winter, and fountains of vernal care now may flow. Springs may flow only in the springtime, after sorrow's hard season has done its work. We become comforters to others. As those who suffer, we experience more deeply the love of ". . . the Father of mercies, and the God of all comfort; Who comforteth us in all our tribulation that we may be able to comfort them which are in any trouble, by the comfort wherewith we ourselves are comforted of God. For as the sufferings of Christ abound in us, so our consolation also aboundeth by Christ. . . . As ye are partakers of the sufferings, so shall ye of the consolations" (2 Corinthians 1:3–5, 7).

Of all the ministries God has entrusted to His people, is any greater than that of suffering? Our Lord Jesus was "a man of sorrows and acquainted with grief." As the suffering Savior and our Great High Priest, He is ". . . touched with the feelings of our infirmities . . ." (Hebrews 4:15). He ceaselessly acts on our behalf ". . . seeing he ever liveth to make intercession for us" (Hebrews 7:25). We are able to engage, in part, in priestly ministry as we enter into suffering. "The ministry of suffering," A. T. Robertson contends, "is one of the blessings of life. It equips us for service in a way that nothing else does or can."[37] Christ calls and encourages us to engage in this blessed ministry to a suffering world.

> There is no anodyne for heart sorrow like ministry to others. If your life is woven with the dark shades of sorrow, do not sit down to deplore in solitude your helpless lot but arise to seek out those who are more miserable than you are.[38]

Soon the suffering will end. Agony does not last forever, although in the dark hours of the soul's Gethsemane, it seems interminable. Jesus our Lord "suffered once." That is all God asks of His children. We will suffer once, albeit the time may seem, as we go through it, like an eternity. The suffering may scale the heights of intensity or plunge us into the abyss of agony, but it will last *only* as long as this life lasts. Then, we will shout ecstatically in victory, "It is finished!" ". . . Weeping may endure for a night, but joy cometh in the morning"

(Psalms 30:5). An eternal day dawns and the faint glimmer of light already greets us playfully in the eastern sky; soon the Daystar will appear and the ". . . Sun of righteousness arise with healing in his wings . . ." (Malachi 4:2). Then God Himself will wipe away all tears, and there will be no more sorrow—no pain—no suffering. Gloriously, we shall be freed from all the fetters, but until then, we suffer "this little while." We grieve for those whom we miss, from whom we are separated, but in the grief, we rest with "blessed assurance" in the "blessed hope." As difficult as we now find it to acknowledge that the gold of God's eternity is being smelted in the furnace of time's suffering, *that* day will reveal the truth of it.

Who does not know that our most sorrowful days have been amongst our best. . . . Stars shine brightest in the long dark nights of winter. . . . God's promises seem to wait for the pressure of pain to trample out their richest juice as in a winepress. Sorrow brings us nearest to the Man of Sorrows, and is the surest passport to His loving sympathy. Only those who sorrow know how tender His comfort can be. It is only as the door shuts upon the joys of earth that the window is opened to the blessedness of the unseen and the eternal. Let sadness cover your face, Jesus will enter the heart and make it glad, for the days in which you have been afflicted, and the years in which you have seen evil.

Is your face sad? Are you passing through bitter and trying experiences? Be of good cheer. Out of the sorrows that make the face sad will come ultimate joy.[39]

7

Prophets Through Pain: The Young Die

A child who cries at the
coffin of his father is
only mature when he has
lived long enough to cry
at the coffin of his son.

Never was a boy crucified
but that the weeping Father
always found the nail-prints
in his own hands.[1]

❧ 7 ❧

Nikos Kazantzakis, the celebrated Greek author, describes three kinds of souls and three kinds of corresponding prayers:

> One: I am a bow in your hands, Lord. Draw me lest I rot.
> Two: Do not overdraw me, Lord. I shall break.
> Three: Overdraw me, and who cares if I break.[2]

With resolve, we pray the first prayer, but soon, timidly, we see ourselves at the breaking point, and we meekly ask for a reprieve. Few, a blessed few, resolutely pray the third prayer. For many of those who do utter that prayer, God takes them at their word. A word of caution to us all: Let us be careful what we say we are willing to give to God—He *may* take it! If we are serious, He *will* take it.

How important is long life? Is longevity a sign of God's favor? Does not the psalmist say, "with long life will I satisfy him . . ."? (Psalms 91:16). Is not long life a promise given to them who honor father and mother? (Deuteronomy 5:16). We see the saints of old who were "gathered unto their people" full of years. How poetically put! Abraham, Isaac, Jacob, David, Solomon, Moses, Joshua, Caleb—all had lived their "three score and ten." Job died at a good old age after his affliction. Surely, many years is an unmistakable sign of God's pleasure in us? If we serve him faithfully and remain loyal to Christ's cause, we will live full, and then mellow and mature enter our eternal home—has he not assured us of this? In the wispy words of William Cullen Bryant, shall we not, "sustained and soothed By an unfaltering trust," pull the draperies of our couch about us and lie down to pleasant dreams?

But we know that does not always happen! Perhaps the reality is *typically* quite the opposite. Will heaven be peopled principally with those who have died in infancy? Is the present alarming abortion rate adding to the population of heaven in proportions beyond those of mature age? The demographic records suggest that, historically, the vast majority of people never survived into adulthood.

God does not reckon time as we do. Nor does He count years and sum them into totals. If a thousand years is as a day to Him and a day as a thousand years (2 Peter 3:8), is it not possible that one day lived in His presence may count more than a century spent apart from Him? On the campus where we lived, an elderly couple were themselves living legends. In fidelity to God and each other, they were exemplars. The husband died the same year Keith died. Keith had not yet reached his seventeenth birthday. The elderly gentleman was ninety-four years old. He was seventy-eight years old when Keith was born! Eight years beyond his allotted time. His life reached its twilight when Keith entered the world. By comparison, Keith's brief moment on the stage of life seemed a twinkling of an eye.

How can sixteen years, most of them in early development, compare to the productive longevity of a patriarch? By all human standards, the one life looked grand, productive, and filled with success. The other life, at best, was just beginning. A flame too soon extinguished. A friend of ours, upon hearing of Keith's illness, said simply over and over: "So young. So young." How true!

There have been those notable lives that, short-lived, have nevertheless distinguished themselves. Occasionally, celebrities attain to notoriety but are soon snuffed out. Sometimes they survive as cult figures, revered by their followers. James Dean, the prototypic angry young man, has retained his hypnotic appeal for this generation of followers, although he died several decades ago. Daily, flocks of devotees make pilgrimages to the home of Elvis Presley, and his memory is kept alive as fans continue to yield homage to him. He died at the age of forty-two, in sad circumstances.

An elite group among God's people saw life not in limited terms of quantity of time but in quality of commitment to Christ. They lived as people whose vision pierced eternity. The dividing line between life and death was not an abrupt one for them. Paul, the apostle, confessed that he had a desire to depart and be with Christ, which was far better (Philippians 1:23). These select saints established as their priority, Christ's presence, whether that involved life or death.

My son, Keith, died at the age of sixteen years. Is it possible that he fulfilled God's purposes for him? Unquestionably, yes! A good pastor friend of ours had told Keith that God would not take him home until he had fulfilled God's purposes here on earth. That has to be true.

Several years ago, the college at which I teach had as its

commencement speaker Paul Little, faculty member at Trinity Divinity School and staff member with Inter-Varsity Christian Fellowship. This successful author and nationally prominent evangelical leader was a key organizer of the initial Congress on Evangelism held in Europe and sponsored by the Billy Graham Association. In his address, Paul took as his text, Acts 13:36: "For David, after he had served his own generation by the will of God, fell on sleep. . . ." He emphasized the significance of the generation in which we live, for that holds God's purpose for us. His address was forceful, inspirational, and backed by the credibility of his own life of devotion. Later that summer, Paul Little was killed in an automobile accident. A respected Christian leader in the prime of life, cut down by a seemingly senseless accident! Could not God have spared Paul Little's life to allow the profit that had accrued from his leadership and service? Would not his family and his calling have benefited, had he remained among us? The answer to these questions and all the others that could legitimately be raised is an unqualified—yes. But God in His sovereignty saw fit to allow the accident to happen. I avoid the use of the word *caused.* God's choice servants do not always fulfill their threescore and ten term allotment.

Dietrich Bonhoeffer died at the age of thirty-nine, one short of the biblical generation of forty. He spent his last years in a Nazi prison. He was executed! He wrote those compelling words that challenge each one of us: "When Christ calls a man, he bids him come and die." The German pastor willingly died rather than renounce his commitment to Christ. He would not substitute "cheap grace" for "costly grace." The consequences of such a compromise, he knew, had eternal significance. When today we speak of Bonhoeffer, it is in reverent tones. We whisper the name of a martyr.

George Gillespie, born in 1613, served several churches in Scotland for nine years. As a representative to the Westminster Assembly in 1643, his persuasiveness played an instrumental part in pleading the cause of the Presbyterians. He apparently suffered ill health, and during his last illness, "he enjoyed little comfort but was strong in the faith of adherence to divine promises. . . . When asked if he had any comfort, he said: 'No, but though the Lord allow me no comfort, yet I will *believe* that my Beloved is mine and that I am his.' "[3] He died at the age of thirty-five.

The great Puritan divine Jonathan Edwards wrote:

[God] has also raised up some eminent persons who have set bright examples of that religion which is taught and prescribed in the Word of God; whose examples have, in the course of divine providence, been set forth to public view. . . . Such an instance we have in the excellent person whose life is published in the following pages.[4]

The person of whom Edwards wrote was the missionary David Brainerd. One of the rare servants of God in the realm of piety and holiness, Brainerd sought an ever closer walk with Christ. He desired that his life would be the instrument to bring the heathen into the fold of the Good Shepherd, so that heaven's host would be increased with worshipers of the Lord Jesus. Brainerd's diary is an adventure in intimacy. With reverence one reads those soul-wrenching cries for holiness and for communion with Christ. A life aflame, daily devoted to the love of God! This saint spent endless hours in prayers and meditation and contemplation upon the glories of Christ. So little of that seems to be part of the church's life today. Brainerd was living on the higher plain—in the rarefied spiritual empyrean where, although on earth, heaven is never nearer.

> But now my soul more frequently desires to die, to be with Christ. O that my soul were rapt in divine love and my longing desires after God increased! . . . I thought, if God would take me to himself now, my soul would exceedingly rejoice. . . . O my blessed God! Let me climb up near to Him and love, and long and plead and wrestle and stretch after him. . . . O come Lord Jesus, Amen.[5]

> I felt weaned from the world. . . . I cannot hope I shall see that glorious day. Everything in this world seems exceedingly vile and little to me. . . .[6]

> I know I long for God and a conformity to His will, in inward purity and holiness ten thousand times more than anything here below.[7]

On the occasion of his twenty-fourth birthday, April 20, Brainerd wrote these words in his journal:

> This day I am twenty four years of age. Oh, how much mercy have I received this year past! How often has God caused His goodness to pass before me! And how poorly have I answered the vows I made this time twelve months to be wholly the Lord's, to be forever devoted to His service. The Lord help me to live more to His glory for the time to come. This has been a sweet, a happy day to me; blessed be God. . . . I want to wear out my life in His service, and for His glory.[8]

Time and time again throughout the journal, we hear the cry after God. Repeated references to his many hours spent in prayer and meditation testify to Brainerd's quest for consecration—yea, for consummation—in Christ. His ministry among the Indians was one of rigor and resolution. His travels drained his meager energies. Sickness was a constant menace, and he refers often in his writings to his infirmities. As his ministry drew to its close, he experienced great weakness and poor health.

> Lord's Day, September 12, 1746. I was so weak I could not preach, nor pretend to ride over to my people in the forenoon. . . . Saturday, September 27. Spent this day, as well as the whole week past, under a great degree of bodily weakness exercised with a violent cough and a considerable fever. . . . I was sometimes scarce able to walk and never able to sit up the whole day, through the week. . . . I had little strength to pray, none to write or read, and scarce any to meditate; but through divine goodness, I could with great composure look death in the face and frequently with sensible joy. Oh, how blessed it is, to be habitually prepared for death. The Lord grant that I may be actually ready also.[9]

Brainerd had prayed that God would not let him outlive his usefulness. His last entries in his diary reflected his anticipation of his homegoing. One entry made by Jonathan Edwards himself records Brainerd's willingness to leave all those he loved, knowing they would be reunited in God's heaven. Edwards's daughter, Jerusha, attended Brainerd during his last illness.

Jerusha, as her father notes, would follow Brainerd into God's presence within the year! She was eighteen years old.

> Dear Jerusha, are you willing to part with me? I am quite willing to part with you; I am willing to part with all my friends; I am willing to part with my dear brother, John, although I love him the best of any creature living. I have committed him and all my friends to God and can leave them with God.[10]

David Brainerd, one of the pure in heart, saw God on Friday, October 9, 1747. He died that day at twenty-nine years of age!

In a highly compelling and emotionally moving book, Ernest Gordon describes the nightmare of a Japanese prison camp in which he and so many other men suffered during World War II. The unspeakable, ghastly horror and atrocities to which the captives were subjected defy description and often belief. But we know the levels of degradation to which man is known to descend. In one profoundly moving incident, Gordon tells about the death of a "young lad," a fellow countryman. The boy was suffering from gangrene, and death was imminent. He was beyond help or hope. Gordon stopped by to see him.

> Large frightened gray eyes stared up at me from an emaciated face. I bent closer. He seemed to recognize me.
> Oh, I'm so glad to see you, sir.
> He managed to sit up.
> I'm glad to see *you,* I replied.

158

Perhaps you don't know me, he said. I arrived with the last draft. I've seen you often, but you probably haven't seen me.

The last draft I remembered only too well. Those who had been sent to us were boys of eighteen. . . . I've been so lonely. I don't know anyone here. It's been a long time since I've seen an Argyll. . . .

It's been hard for you hasn't it?

Awfully hard, he nodded with self-consciousness. I've become terribly depressed. I suppose because I'm scared. I'm so scared at times I can't think.

What are you scared of?

Oh—scared about the Nips—and scared that I'm going to die.

What could I say? I knew I didn't have a chance because of the advanced state of his gangrene. I looked at him, lying there so lonely and so young, and said the only thing I could think of.

We'll help you not to be scared. We'll stay by you.

That seemed to ease his mind.

Thank you sir, that's good to know.

He gave me an engaging boyish grin. I got up. . . .

My mother and dad will miss me. I'm the only one they have and they'll be so lonely when I don't come back.

He gave a little sigh.

It's hard to be young and have to die. I don't even know what this war is all about.

Here, let me read something that may help. I spoke the words evenly, pretending to be in more control of my emotions than I actually was. I had brought my Bible with me. I opened its torn pages and in the dim light of the hut, I began to read those words that had brought solace to countless souls before him. "Yea, though I walk through the valley of the shadow of death, I will fear no evil: for thou art with me; thy rod and thy staff they comfort me."

I looked at him. He was lying quietly. I turned to another passage.

"I am the resurrection and the life; he that believeth in me, though he were dead, yet shall he live: And whosoever liveth and believeth in me shall never die. Believest thou this?"

I put the Bible down. His gray eyes were far away. He was listening within himself—to the message these words had brought. After a bit he turned his gaze to mine and said with perfect calm,

Everything is going to be all right.

Yes, I said, nodding, everything is going to be all right. . . .

It's all right. I'm glad it's all right, he whispered. There was a look of trust and hope on his face as he said this.

Yes, my son, it's all right, I assured him. God our father is with us. He is very near. My voice was husky. I know he is. The sigh the boy gave was not sad but confident.

Still holding his hand, I prayed.

"Our father which art in heaven, Hallowed be thy name."

His eyes were closed. But as I watched his face I could see his lips repeating the words with me.

". . .thy kingdom come. . . ."

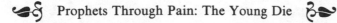

The lamp grew dim then burned more brightly.
"...Thy will be done in earth as it is in heaven...."
His lips no longer moved. His breath started coming
in great sobbing gasps.
They ceased. He was quiet—with the quietness of
death.[11]

I read the words slowly, meditatively. A life of eighteen,
barely on the brink of manhood, now gone. Death came for
him in the most unhospitable way. A prisoner of war—a war
the purpose of which he did not even know. In a foreign land
without the presence of parents, parents who would live with
pain's memory. Death certainly did not come with dignity. But
beside the lad, there was a man who knew Christ and knew
Him in the confines of the prison camp.

My own son became the victim of a war of which he was
scarcely aware: the cosmic conflict caused by the forces of evil
who had opened the Pandora's box of affliction by disobedi-
ence to God. One of the dreaded evils that came out of that
box answered to the name *cancer*. Understandably Keith felt
fear. Fear of something about which he knew so little. He had
to die alone. We all do. Yet he died so young. But in his youth
he knew his Creator and Redeemer, and I could be there with
him and read the very Scriptures Ernest Gordon read to the
lad from Scotland. And to pray the very prayer that Gordon
prayed. To listen to the painful sobs and then see the stillness.
To see death come for the very young. And to know with ut-
most assurance that God's will is being done on earth.

Never do we fully realize the frailty and briefness of life's
flickering flame until we see the candle about to be snuffed out.
We seem so strong. We feel we will last forever and that things
will continue on the way they have been. How easy to become

settled in—to feel the ease that the rhythm of life's unaltered beat brings. We are gleefully content to enjoy things full and fat. Then without warning, circumstances jettison us from our secure moorings and set us adrift.

> Moab hath been at ease from his youth, and he hath settled on his lees, and hath not been emptied from vessel to vessel, neither hath he gone into captivity: therefore his taste remained in him, and his scent is not changed.
>
> Jeremiah 48:11

We become stale and sterile when we stay too long in one place and one position. Often God jolts us from our complacency, to remind us that things do not remain the same. Life will have its ending and for some, it will come all too quickly.

> Not yet thou knowest what I do
>   O feeble child of earth,
> Whose life is but to angel view
>   The morning of thy birth!
> The smallest leaf, the simplest flower,
>   The wild bee's honey-cell
> Have lessons of My love and power
>   Too hard for thee to spell.
>
> Thou knowest not how I uphold
>   The little thou dost scan;
> And how much less canst thou unfold
>   My universal plan,
> Where all the mind can grasp of space
>   is but a grain of sand;

The time thy boldest thought can trace
  One ripple on the strand.

Not yet thou knowest how I bid
  Each passing hour entwine;
Its grief or joy, its hope or fear
  in one great love-design;
Nor how I lead thee through the night
  By many a various way,
Still upward to unclouded light
  and onward to the day.[12]

Frances Ridley Havergal was a talented young lady affectionately called "Christ's sweet singer." She lost her mother at the age of twelve, but through the loss, she gained strength in Christ. Noted as a woman of charm and creativity, she demonstrated her gifts as a soloist and a prolific writer of poetry and hymns. All her life, however, constant colds and ill health plagued her. On more than one occasion, it looked as though her frail frame could no longer endure. Miraculously, during periods of infirmity, she authored hymns, books, and corresponded with friends. In May, 1879, she passed into the presence of the Lord about whom she had sung and whom she extolled in her hymns and verse. She died at the age of forty-two! Her rich legacy of hymnody remains today a bountiful blessing in inspiration and comfort to all who join in worship. Her songs grace the pages of hymnbooks the world over. Her poem "The Right Way" eloquently testifies to her faith in the Lord Jesus in the face of conflict and pain.

Lord, is it still the right way, though I cannot
  see Thy face,

163

Though I do not feel Thy presence and Thine
    all-sustaining grace?
Can even this be leading through the bleak and
    sunless wild
To the City of Thy holy rest, the mansions un-
    defiled?

Lord, is it still the right way? A while ago I
    passed
Where every step seemed thornier and harder
    than the last;
Where bitterest disappointment and only ach-
    ing sorrow
Carved day by day a weary cross, renewed with
    every morrow.

The heaviest end of that strange cross I knew
    was laid on Thee;
So I could still press on secure of Thy deep
    sympathy.
Our upward path may well be steep, else how
    were patience tried?
I knew it was the right way, for it led me to Thy
    side.

But now I wait alone amid dim shadows dank
    and chill;
All moves and changes round me, but I seem
    standing still;
Or every feeble footstep I urge towards the
    light
Seems but to lead me farther into the silent
    night.

I cannot hear thy voice, Lord! dost Thou still
    hear my cry?
I cling to Thy assurance that Thou art ever
    nigh;
I know that Thou art faithful; I trust, but can-
    not see,
That it is still the right way by which Thou
    leadest me. . . .

Is this Thy chosen training for some future task
    unknown?
Is it that I may learn to rest upon Thy word
    alone?
Whate'er it be, oh! leave me not, fulfill Thou
    every hour
The purpose of Thy goodness, and the work of
    faith with power.[13]

Geoffrey Bull, a missionary to Tibet who suffered imprisonment for four years under the Chinese communists, relates this
incident in his profoundly challenging book, *The Sky Is Red.*

In the year 1662 when many godly servants of our
Lord Jesus Christ were bitterly persecuted for their
faithfulness to the Word of God, Joseph Allein was
on his way to preach to the believers meeting at
Luppitt near Tauton when he was summarily ar-
rested and taken to Ilchester prison. ... From his
prison cell, he wrote, "know, dear Christians, that
the bonds of the Gospel are not tedious through
grace unto us; that Christ is a Master worth suffering

for . . . that Christ's prison is better than the world's paradise . . . that the influence of heaven, and shines of God's countenance are sufficient to lighten the darkest dungeon."

His wife knew this was no mere pious language for she testified that, "All the time of his health, he did rise constantly at or before 4 o'clock, and on Sabbath earlier, if he did awake. He would be much troubled if he heard any smiths, or shoemakers or such tradesmen at work at their trades before he was in his duties with God; saying to me often, 'O, how this noise shames me! Doth not my master desire more than theirs.' " Writing of his heart's desiring he says, "That in all I do, whether sacred or civil actions, still may I be doing but one work, and driving on one design, that God may be pleased by me and glorified in me. . . ."

This devoted disciple of our Lord Jesus Christ died at the age of 35 just three years after his first arrest and largely on account of the privations he suffered in prison.[14]

Who will ever know of the many who have died in prison—in severe privation and *seemingly* prematurely? God knows, and the value of a life, by these circumstances, is underscored. Scripture reminds us to number our days, but the *value* of our days God alone can determine. We will leave the tallying to the One whose formula for determining such includes eternity's factor. Time alone can never give the true estimate. Little becomes much when God is in it!

Robert Murray McCheyne was born in Edinburgh, Scotland, in May, 1813. He had a brilliant intellect and distinguished himself in all his academic pursuits. He matriculated at Edinburgh University when he was fourteen years old. The death of his brother, David, at the age of twenty-seven, had a profound impact upon Robert's life. The godly example of the brother whom he loved dearly produced a noticeable change in McCheyne's own search for holiness. There are numerous references in his writings to the death of his brother and his reaction to it.

> On this morning last year came the first overwhelming blow to my worldliness: how blessed to me, Thou, O God, only knowest, who has made it so. . . . Pray for me, that I may be holier and wiser—less like myself, and more like my heavenly Master; that I may not regard my life, if so be that I may finish my course with joy. This day eleven years ago, I lost my loved and loving brother, and began to see a Brother who cannot die.[15]

McCheyne's pastoral and personal letters are throbs from his heart as well as thoughts from his head. The tender tones that characterize his shepherd sensitivity reflect his personal nearness to Christ's heart. He writes as one who is in consonance with the very heartbeat of Jesus. His soul felt burdened for his flock. On his travels to the Holy Land, McCheyne kept up a steady stream of correspondence, exhorting the saints to stay close to the Savior. His compassion seems remarkable for one so young. Often we think the cords of sympathy are tenderized over time. Perhaps the very opposite is true. Maybe as we move from childhood, we became toughened and lose the elasticity of love.

McCheyne had written a letter in response to a young boy

identified simply as J. T. In this epistle, McCheyne exhorted the lad to "go alone and look up to Jesus, who died to wash us from our sins, and say, *'Wash me.'* " Shortly after, the little boy to whom McCheyne wrote died. In a letter to the boy's brother, McCheyne answered gently:

> I did not think I was to have answered your kind letter in the time of bitter grief. . . . I saw your dear little brother on his dying bed, and indeed I could not believe he was dying, except that his calm eye was directed to the hills of Immortality, and he seemed already to breathe some of the atmosphere of the world of sinless joy. I do trust and believe that he was a saved boy. You know I am rather slow of coming to this conviction and not fond of speaking when I have not good evidence; but here, I think God has not left us in doubt.
>
> At Blairgowrie he used several times to speak to me about divine things, and the tear would gather in his eye when he said that he feared that he had never been brought to Jesus. . . . But now he was quite different. . . . Over and over he told me that he was not afraid to die, for Christ had died. . . . He seemed tranquil and happy, even when the pain came on in his head and made him knit his brows. . . . He is not lost but gone before and we shall soon put off this clay cottage also. . . . Your dear little brother lies like a marble statue in the peaceful sleep of death, till Jesus' voice shall waken him. Happy boy! . . . The days of his mourning are ended, and his eternity of love and holy joy begun.[16]

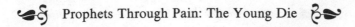

When McCheyne reached his twenty-first birthday, he wrote in his diary: "Oh, how long and worthlessly I have lived, Thou only knowest! Neff died in his thirty-first year. When shall I?"[17]

McCheyne died in 1843, not having quite reached his thirtieth birthday!

> Next morning, at a quarter past nine, he expired, and all that day nothing was to be heard in the houses around but lamentation and great mourning and as a friend in that neighborhood wrote, "In passing along the high road, you saw the faces of everyone swollen with weeping."[18]

Dundee and all Scotland—indeed, all the world—have been influenced by the life of a godly man who did not live beyond three decades. The quality of his life and ministry are evident in his impact on others. His journals reveal the movements of a man who learned quite early in life the secret of living close to Christ. Tourists who have visited his memorial in Scotland have remarked upon the stains on the chair on which he sat and before which he kneeled in prayer. Those stains, they have been told, were the tears that McCheyne shed so often as he talked with his Lord.

My son, Keith, was an avid fan of the film, *Chariots of Fire*. I confess that I shared his enthusiasm. We saw that motion picture a dozen times, and each time we viewed it, it seemed refreshingly new. Together we sat in the darkened theater, enthralled at the sight of a man who ran to please God and who remained undaunted in his convictions. Eric Liddell, the subject of the film, has emerged as a hero to a generation seeking for and so desperately needing them. Amazingly a man who lay in obscurity for over fifty years suddenly surfaced and found a ready audience for his dramatic story.

The simplicity of Liddell's life and his courage to oppose convention form the basis for the plot of the film. A man of great ability who would not compromise his principles is a rarity, particularly in this present age of opportunism. Eric Liddell combined in himself the commitment to excellence in athletics and an unfailing devotion to Jesus Christ. Keith had virtually memorized the entire script, and the dialogue would weave itself into his talk.

"Eric's special—he's precious," Jenny, Eric's sister, would say. Keith would feign the Scottish accent.

"You feel elation when the winner breaks the tape. Especially if you got a bet on 'im." Keith would let this line come up from the back of his throat.

Eric Liddell's accomplishment at the 1924 Olympics became legendary. He won the 400 meters in record time, an event for which he scarcely trained. He became Scotland's most celebrated athlete. However, at the apex of his career, with the athletic world ready to fawn all over him, he walked away from fame and possible fortune and became a missionary in China, the country in which he had grown up.

A recent biographer asks the questions:

> Who was this man, Eric Liddell? What kind of person was it who could compete so effectively, yet turn down the chance of Olympic glory so effortlessly. . . . who could shrug off all the super star adulation and head off for China as casually as if he were popping off for a week-end in London . . . above all who had

such a shattering impact on all who met him that nobody, nobody at all ever had a bad word to say of him? For children and adults alike adored Eric Liddell. Even now, those who remember him have only extravagant praise. . . . When he died, all Scotland mourned.[19]

Eric Liddell was taken prisoner by the Japanese, along with other missionaries, and he spent his internment at Weihsien. During his camp confinement, he continued to manifest the graciousness of Christ. The testimonies to his life of witness abound.

When Eric died, one of the women in the camp, a Russian prostitute, told my mother that Eric Liddell was the only man who had ever done anything for her and not wanted to be repaid in kind. . . . It didn't matter what walk of life a person came from, Eric wouldn't judge anybody.[20]

Eric's biographer records another illustration of his consistent life from the book, *Courtyard of the Happy Way*.

Eric Liddell was "the most outstanding Weihsien personality . . . quiet-spoken and with a permanent smile, Eric was the finest Christian man I have ever had the privilege of meeting.[21]

His life shone out, a white shaft of purity and consistency in circumstances that brought out the worst in people. Whether in the arena of Olympic contests or in the infamous internment camp of cruelty, Eric Liddell was a man of unflinching courage and unwavering devotion.

> What they keep coming back to again and again, these people, is the way he *lived* his Christianity. Eric is portrayed as the Christ-figure here at the camp just as much as he was among the Chinese in Siachang. He befriends the prostitute, and the despised businessman; he carries coal for the weak and teaches the young; he gets ready to sell his gold watch and tears up his sheets for hockey sticks. And yet he is the same Eric . . . looking extremely ordinary and nothing special at all.[22]

The darling of Scotland's sports world—the man who could have had society at his feet and could have profited from his justly deserved fame, chose, unhesitatingly and unceremoniously, to sail to China and give his life for Christ in service for others. His life ended in the Japanese internment camp.

His last words uttered were: "Annie, it's complete surrender."[23] Eric became comatose and never recovered consciousness. He died on February 21, 1945, of an apparent brain tumor. So characteristically, he died inconspicuously, at the age of forty-three, not by the barbarity of the Japanese prison camp but by an inoperable tumor.

I sat in the library at the King's College, sprawled in one of the few easy chairs. I flipped through the magazines, discarding them quickly. I reached for a copy of the *Philadelphia Inquirer* and read with keen interest the story of five young men who had been speared to death in Ecuador and whose bodies lay lifeless on the beach. The year was 1956, and the five dead men were missionaries who had gone to bring the gospel to the Indian tribes in the area. One of the five, Jim Elliot, came from Portland, Oregon. That name became legendary in the annals of martyrdom, and that life and death influenced a generation for God.

I never cease to marvel as I read the diaries and journals of Jim Elliot. Such maturity and spiritual perception in the life of such a young man! His college years, although filled with the normal routine of youth, were, nevertheless, saturated with a sense of the Spirit's purpose and planning. Eager to devote himself to the service of Christ, Jim Elliot saw his college life as part of the master plan of preparation. His involvement in the wrestling team afforded him opportunities to test his limits of endurance. The skill and discipline of the wrestler developed his capacities for the wrestlings within his own soul. Like Jacob at Peniel, his soul fought with the Invisible One—the angel of the dark night. The hobble of humility and the halting that ever after marked Jacob out as one with whom God had prevailed gave him, paradoxically, power with God and with men. His single-souled quest became service for his Lord. How willingly Jim forwent the legitimate pleasures of youth to channel himself into the narrow, tightly drawn course of missionary service. Into missionary service he went! In 1952, Jim sailed to Ecuador and served there until January 8, 1956. On that day, along with his four fellow missionaries, the people to whom he had come to minister slaughtered him. Jim Elliot was twenty-nine years old. Did this young man who so willingly gave himself to Christ have a premonition that his life would be a short one? He certainly did not seek a long life. His journals testify to that.

There is no longer an inheritance for me down here. I've been bought by the labors of that great Shepherd who came from afar to gain me as His bride. Lead on, Lord, whatever God's command is or wherever He may lead, I am now ready to go.[24]

God, I pray, light these idle sticks of my life and may I burn up for thee. Consume my life, My God, for it is Thine. I seek not a long life but a full one like yours, Lord Jesus.[25]

Lord, I know Thou art with me, but I fear that because my life is barren for Thee so much of the time, that You gain little glory from being with me. I pray Thee, make my way prosperous, not that I achieve high station, but that my life might be an exhibit to the value of knowing God. Vindicate Thyself through me.[26]

Father, take my life, yea my blood, if Thou wilt, and consume it with Thine enveloping fire. I would not save it, for it is not mine to save. Have it, Lord, have it all. Pour out my life as an oblation for the world. Blood is only of value as it flows before Thine altars.[27]

In one way or another, I would die. Either take me to be with Thee, Savior or put out the life of this old man as I draw near Thee in the flesh. Consume me, Fiery Lover, as Thou dost choose.[28]

Am I ignitible? God deliver me from the dread asbestos of "other things." Saturate me with the oil of the Spirit that I may be a *flame*. But flame is transient, often short-lived. Canst thou bear this, my soul, short life? In me swells the Spirit of the Great

Short-Lived, whose zeal for God's house consumed
Him, and He has promised baptism with the Spirit
and with fire. "Make me Thy fuel, flame of God."[29]

Son of Man, I feel it would be best if I should be
taken now to thy home. I dread causing Thee shame
at thy appearing.[30]

Keith had been dead for less than a month, and the pain we
suffered still pierced into the tender spot of our souls. "The
fractures of sorrow" had become cavernous fissures into which
all feeling had begun to fall. Our church had a meeting of pas-
tors from the region, which required overnight accommodations. My wife and I volunteered Keith's vacant room. We
agreed to have two of the men stay with us, but after the evening service, only one pastor was assigned. The writer to the
Hebrews tell us to be hospitable, because some may be enter-
taining "angels unawares." We came close to that verse that
evening.

The kindly gentleman assigned to us was a blessing from
God. We discovered as the evening progressed, as we sat
drinking tea, that we shared a number of friends and acquain-
tances. He was originally from the Philadelphia area, and so
was I. We spent the evening in nostalgic reflection. He then
asked us how we were feeling since Keith's death. We learned
that the local pastor had shared that with him. Soon that
brother began unfolding something about his own life and
shared how he had lost his own daughter in an accident. She
was a college student, killed in an automobile crash—at
twenty-two.

On the verge of life, young and enterprising and so promising, these lives are no longer on *this earth*. To use Shakespeare's quaint phrase, they have "shuffled off this mortal

coil." Although they expended preparation and study and effort to get ready for the big task of life—to live in the adult world—that world never came. So soon snuffed out! A frail flame! Ernest Gordon cites some poetry written by an unknown English lad who reflected on his own brevity.

> What shall I think when I am called to die?
>   Shall I not find too soon my life has ended?
> The years, too quickly, have hastened by
>   With so little done of all that I intended.
>
> There were so many things I'd meant to try
>   So many contests I had hoped to win
> And lo, the end approaches just as I
>   Was thinking of preparing to begin.[31]

Preparing to begin! Keith had prepared for sixteen years: He devoted himself to his schoolwork and consistently made the honor roll; he practiced his trumpet, gaining skill and competence; he was an inveterate reader; he had developed refinement and character. Surely, such qualities would be immensely useful in this world. Assuredly, God would recognize the need for these young lives in this world where evil so often prevails and the boorish and egocentric dominate. The participation in the world of these lives of quality would doubtless elevate and enhance the quality of life. But no—it is not to be. Jim Elliot, with lofty vision through eternity's lens, corrects such estimations of this limited life:

> I must not think it strange if God takes in youth
>   those whom I should have kept on earth till they

were older. God is peopling eternity, and I must not restrict Him to old men and women.[32]

Why do we not see that lives lived in God's purpose and for His glory have eternal significance? Youth is *not* wasted on the young if that youth is dedicated to God's glory, whether it be by life or death. We tend to assume that by the criterion of age, old age, God chooses and that *only* the elderly have known God's full blessing and have been used in His service. But these "great cloud of witnesses" all demonstrated that years alone do not constitute the key to productivity and blessing. And does not the very person of the Lord Jesus Christ boldly demonstrate that God's will is perfectly completed in the prime of life? Our Lord for thirty years lived His life in obscurity before man (although not before God). "Thou art my beloved Son; in thee I *was* [Greek aorist tense] well pleased" (Luke 3:22). Upon that One who was from all eternity and who lived in Nazareth the Father made this heavenly pronouncement. The cruel death of the cross cut him down at the tender age of thirty-three years. In the full bloom of manhood, when His creative powers and potentials had just reached their apex, our Lord was crucified.

To the unbeliever, this death looked like a waste of a life. In today's marketplace of youth-oriented culture, this appears as nothing less than spoilage. With Judas, the world would say, "Why such a waste?" Mary's alabaster box would do more good if it were slowly emptied and its contents allowed to perfume the room sparingly; that is the crowd's consensus. But God gladly breaks the vase of His Son's vital and efficacious sacrifice *at once,* and in the prime time of His person as Man, He dies on the cross. Was not the Lord aware of this interference into His own life? Did He not in His human sensitivity wonder at it all? The psalmist anticipates His words and wonder:

> He weakened my strength in the way; he shortened my days. I said, O my God, take me not away in the midst of my days. . . .
>
> Psalms 102:23, 24

But in response to this entreaty of His Son, God replies:

> . . .Thy years are throughout all generations. Of old hast thou laid the foundation of the earth: and the heavens are the work of thy hands. They shall perish, but thou shalt endure: yea, all of them shall wax old like a garment; as a vesture shalt thou change them, and they shalt be changed. But thou art the same, and thy years shall have no end.
>
> Psalms 102:24–27

The One who died was and is the Eternal One. Almighty God of never-ending days has become Man who died and now lives in resurrected life. "I am he that liveth, and was dead; and, behold, I am alive for evermore . . ." (Revelation 1:18). At the peak of His manhood Christ was resurrected, and His never-dying body prototypes the resurrected bodies which we shall have: "Who shall change our vile body, that it may be fashioned like unto his glorious body . . ." (Philippians 3:21). In His Resurrection, the Lord Jesus has "the dew of thy youth" (Psalms 110:3). His locks "are bushy, and black as a raven" (Song of Solomon 5:11). In the full vigor of the timelessness of eternity He stands astride the ages without a sign of wear or age. His brow is without wrinkle. His strength knows no slacking. In resurrection virility, He will lead His people untiringly throughout the ages of the ages.

Heaven will be peopled with the eternally young in the fullness of strength and in full command of undiminished faculties and senses. The resurrected, ascended and reigning Lord assures that old age is banished and the young who have departed fit so well into His Father's house. As verses from the hymn sung at my son's memorial service so aptly express:

> Jesus lives, and so shall I.
>   Death! thy sting is gone forever:
> He, who deigned for me to die
>   Lives, the bands of death to sever.
> He shall raise me with the just:
> Jesus is my Hope and Trust.
>
> Jesus lives, and death is now
>   But my entrance into glory.
> Courage! then, my soul, for thou
>   Hast a crown of life before thee;
> Thou shalt find thy hopes were just—
> Jesus is the Christian's Trust.[33]

8

Heaven Bound

You never write of heaven
  Though you write of heavenly themes;
You never paint the glory
  But in reflected gleams!
My pencil only pictures
  What I have known and seen:
How can I tell the joys that dwell
  Where I have never been? . . .

To whom all sound is silence,
  The dumb man might impart
The spirit-winging marvels
  of Handel's sacred art.
But never, sister, never
  Was told by mortal breath

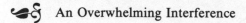

What they behold, o'er whom hath rolled
 The one dark wave of death. . . .

Our fairest dream can never
 Outshine that holy light
Our noblest thought can never soar
 Beyond that word of might.
Our whole anticipation,
 Our Master's best reward,
Our crown of bliss, is summed in this—
 "Forever with the Lord."[1]

❧ 8 ❧

Heaven is a perplexing subject. The Bible says so little about it. Is that because so little *can* be said? Certainly not because it is *not* worth saying! The vision does not translate well into human language. The first vision given to the apostle John, as he records it in the Revelation, left him speechless! He became like a dead man (Revelation 1:17). Paul, the apostle of magnificent revelations, was ". . . caught up into the third heaven . . . caught up into paradise and heard unspeakable words which it is not lawful for a man to utter" (2 Corinthians 12:2, 4).

Heaven must defy description! Therefore, the Scriptures provide so precious little information about it. God has not chosen to satisfy our curiosity, although He leaves hints and harbingers sprinkled throughout His Word. When, in human terms, we attempt to convey something of exquisite delight, we quite naturally use the word *heaven!* Experiences and anticipations that transcend human communication or elaboration must be assigned to an incommunicable category. So we do, although admittedly only in faint approximation, entertain ideas about a place so unlike this place that we invest it with all the allurement of our most grandiose fantasies.

But heaven is not fantasy—some airy, ethereal "*un*-place." Nor can we describe it *simply* as our projection of wishes. It is not a utopia in the literal, "not-a-place" sense. Poetically, metaphorically, we may talk about our paradises and conjure up imagery to express the "unlike earth" character of our dreams and desires, but the biblical heaven of God's presence has solid substance. Heaven is not earth. But may not heaven be akin to earth? We are told, "In the beginning God created the heavens and the earth" (Genesis 1:1). The divine record shows that God had them in mind together, although He created them as distinct elements and the times may have been different. God's creative design derives from His own creative consistency. God is never fragmented or unbalanced. Order and symmetry exist in His plan—a *cosmos* of order, not a *chaos* of disorder. God never intended the blight of sin to mar His perfection. He promises the renewal, restoration, indeed, the regeneration of His new order.

So earth, even in its cursed state (and woefully more than we might think) does, in part, tell us about God's true intention. The world in which we live is a *part,* continuous with the whole of God's creation. This planet, although now in rebellion, permits us pleasures in senses and in soul that must mirror (but darkly) the perfection God intended and will ultimately effect.

Language, with its limitations, is not wasted in describing the realm of celestial delight. The nomenclature of the scientist becomes of little use in moving our spirits, although we can marvel at the spectacle of this creation as science provides us with a lens through which to *peer.* But we need the poet's perspective to disentangle ourselves from the confining cobwebs of sense, and the *seer* best offers the creative clarity. In Scripture, the language employed in describing heaven is symbolic and transcendent. However, the symbols seem clearly earth oriented. We need no "tongues of angels" to talk about the things "which God has prepared for them that love Him." In our spirits the Spirit of God tells us something of the inexpressible glory that awaits us *There* and the bliss which those now *There* enjoy.

I can no longer think about heaven without thinking about my son's presence. When Keith lived on earth, I saw clear, incontrovertible truth that he was *here*. I saw him, talked with him, and through all the human channels of earth, we conversed. In heaven, he became more vitally alive that he was here, freed from the limitations that this body of corruption placed upon him. His body here (as is ours) was essential for this environment. We cannot function on earth without a "natural body," which Paul describes as "carthy" (1 Corinthians 15:44, 48). Interaction in this sphere of the sensory, in this realm of the present reality, requires bodies suitable for it. When we move too far away from earth (to the moon, for example) we need equipment that will accommodate that environment: Weighted shoes to compensate for the lack of gravity and oxygen to compensate for the atmosphere deprivation become critically important. Once, however, we move into the realm of God's abode, we need a radically different body, a "spiritual body," which God has promised will be ours at the final resurrection. Until that day, I assume we are given suitable accommodations for our spirits when we depart the life on this earth. We become not angels but "equal unto the angels" in that we cannot "die any more" (Luke 20:36). We enter into a new sphere of service, and a transformation occurs that allows us to function within the new, heavenly environment.

Heaven cannot be a place of "soul sleep." Those who have left this life here do not lie in some sort of seraphic, suspended animation! Once someone asked me to demonstrate biblically that when believers die they are indeed alive with God. I referred to the oft-quoted words of the apostle Paul "to be absent from the body, and to be present with the Lord" (2 Corinthians 5:8). The rejoinder to my reference was: that does not, however, say we will be *alive* with God! Then I referred to the words the Lord Jesus quoted to the rationalist Sadducees—the very words Jehovah had said to Moses: ". . . the Lord, the God of Abraham, and the God of Isaac, and the God of Jacob. For he is not a God of the dead, but of the living: for all live unto him" (Luke 20:37, 38). At this very instant, Abraham, Isaac, and Jacob live in God's very presence. "All the saints of all the ages in their glory will be there." And my son, Keith, is there. We who are alive on this earth are the limited ones, partial in our knowledge and understanding. Heaven is a place of vitality—of dynamic life, of grand and cosmic perspective! It is a place of present awareness, of magnificent panoramas that on earth are obscured by "earth-borne clouds," which arise.

In one of his books, Alan Redpath, erstwhile pastor of Moody Memorial Church, relates an experience that helps illustrate this point. When Redpath was in London, a friend visited him, and he took his friend on a sightseeing tour of the city. Unfortunately, on that day the legendary fog of London had settled in thickly. Much of the sights of the city lay buried beneath a shroud of fog. When the two men arrived at the magnificent Cathedral of Saint Paul's and admired the architecture and ornateness of the work of Sir Christopher Wren, they climbed the stairs to the very top of the tower. As they emerged from the stairwell, a spectacular sight greeted them. They stood above the fog, and the sun shone radiantly against a sky of lustrous blue. Below—the fog! Above—the firmament! So heaven can only be viewed from such a peak. We can, at best, only approximate its dimensions and designs. It remains beyond description in its grandeur. But assuredly, in this place the full life and love of God abound. In God's presence, the psalmist proclaims, ". . . is fulness of joy; at thy right hand, there are pleasures for evermore" (Psalms 16:11).

I once heard a radio preacher say that God left so much about heaven unsaid, because if He revealed what it is like, an epidemic of suicides would ensue. People would not resist going there. That may stretch the point, but the Lord Jesus and the apostle Paul both viewed heaven and hinted at its glory. The Lord prayed that we might be with Him where He is and behold His glory, which the Father had given Him (John 17:24).

C. S. Lewis more than any other person whose works I have read approaches the poetic apprehension of heaven. Theological discussions of heaven remain limited, although useful. The imagination, sanctified musings, alone come close to what we intuitively feel heaven is. Heaven satisfies each person's idiosyncratic desires, and the eternal dwelling is tailored by God to fit the peculiar design of our souls.

> Your soul has a curious shape because it is a hollow made to fit a particular swelling in the infinite contours of the divine substance, or a key to unlock one of the doors in the house with many mansions.[2]

Heaven is commodious and accommodating yet clearly unencumbered with untidy traffic of this crowded planet. Lewis amusingly described it as bigger inside than it is outside. It is a place—*the* place where God Himself dwells, and in His presence there is no defilement.

> When we see the face of God we shall know that we
> have always known it. He has been a party to, has
> made, sustained and moved moment by moment
> within all our earthly experiences of innocent love.
> All that was true love ... even on earth, far more
> His than ours and ours only because His.[3]

Sheldon Vanauken recalls that in one of his meetings with C. S. Lewis in England, they talked about death or, more exactly, "awakening after death."

> Whatever it would be like, we thought, our response
> to it would be "Why, of course! Of *course* it's like
> this. How else could it have possibly been."[4]

When Keith was dying, we talked about heaven. What would it be like? The prospect of the unexperienced is always frightening, even when we know something about it. Heaven we have not experienced, but the loving God we have; therefore, the fright that accompanies death need not terrify us. If we are honest, we must admit the prospect of the grand passage from this world into that one does not occur to us without an accompanying tinge of fright. As we thought of its irretrievability it gave both Keith and me a fright. I assured Keith that God our Father was loving and kind and that heaven, which awaited him, would be indeed a hospitable place.

> Most of us know that when we came into *this* world,
> we were not unexpected and we were not unwel-

comed. Loving hands had made joyous preparation for our coming and warm arms held us tenderly against a warm bosom. Will our Heavenly Father be less kind to us than our earthly mother?[5]

"Dad," Keith said to me. "Will God be like you?"

My son knew beyond any possible doubt that I loved him and that I would have done whatever needed to be done for him. My delight was in delighting him. Could God, the Father of the lights, from whom every good and perfect gift comes, do less?

Soon, in God's good time, we'll be united again, I assured Keith. Thank God that He has planned a reunion and a never-parting eternity for us. The shadow of our love will give way to full sunshine.

As Keith lay there, subdued and pensive, fully conscious that our earthly ties would very soon be severed, I knew that the greater grief, after he was gone, would fall to me.

"I'll have to wait for you to join me, then, won't I, Dad?" he said. "It'll seem like a long time without you."

"When my time comes to move on to heaven, my son," I told him solemnly, "you'll be there to greet me. The Lord will welcome me, and He'll say, 'There's someone here who wants to be the first to see you.' And it'll be you! Then I'll say: 'Keith, how has it been? How's heaven?' And you'll say, 'Oh, Dad, it's been glorious. I can't describe it. You'll just have to experience it yourself.' Then I'll say to you: 'Keith, how long has it been now? five years? ten years? twenty years? You've been in heaven that long.' Then you'll look at me somewhat puzzled, and you'll say: 'Dad, you don't understand. I just arrived myself!'"

Heaven is a place of the perpetual present. No time and

delay and disappointment remain. Experience is fresh and vivid, always lived in the electrifying present of God's timelessness. How unnecessary clocks and chronometers and calendars would seem there, where space and separation vanish. In heaven all converges and separations of life are banished.

Do the "departed" know of our affairs? If we can contemplate them, certainly God permits them the privilege of our experiences. It is the relationships, after all, that are the enduring realities. When Jesus resurrected Lazarus, He returned him to the relationships in the home in Bethany, and the widow of Nain's son went back to his mother. The relationships of love begun here on earth, persisting here on earth, must doubtless persist in heaven. "Verily I say unto you, Whatsoever ye shall bind on earth shall be bound [shall have been bound] in heaven . . ." (Matthew 18:18).

> But the eternal distinctness of each soul—the secret which makes of the union between each soul and God a species in itself—will never abrogate the law that forbids ownership in heaven. As to its fellow-creatures, each soul, we suppose, will be eternally engaged in giving away to all the rest that which it receives. . . . For in self-giving, if anywhere, we touch the rhythm not only of all creation but of all being.[6]

Heaven is heavenly. The relationships and fellowships begun faintly on earth will, in the rarefied, ethereal air of God's breathing space, flower ecstatically into full fruition. They will become incomparably more superb than ever we can imagine. There, in a suitable environment, a suitable habitation for life to grow and flourish, the life of love will vigorously and vibrantly flourish without deformity in the dwelling place of God.

> Think of stepping on shore and finding it
>   heaven
> or taking hold of a hand and finding it God's,
> or breathing new air and finding it celestial,
> or feeling invigorated and finding it immortal-
>   ity;
> of passing through a tempest to a new and un-
>   known ground;
> of waking up well and happy and finding it
>   home.[7]

9

Metaphors of Mercy

And all men are idolators, crying unheard
To senseless idols, if Thou take them at their
    word.
And all men in their praying, self-deceived, ad-
    dress
One that is not (so saith that old rebuke) unless
Thou, of mere grace, appropriate, and to Thee
    divert
Men's arrows, all at hazard aimed, beyond des-
    ert.

Take not, oh Lord, our literal sense, but in Thy
    great
Unbroken speech our halting metaphor trans-
    late.[1]

This I recall to my mind, therefore have I hope. It is
of the Lord's mercies that we are not consumed, be-

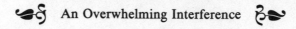

cause his compassions fail not. They are new every morning: great is thy faithfulness.

Lamentations 3:21–23

⤳ 9 ⤲

In 1959, I met him in the quaint town of Ocean Grove, New Jersey. A small man with wool-white hair and dancing eyes, his face glowed like Moses' on the Mount. Although in his tenth decade of life, still he retained his keen mind and quickness of wit. He died within the year. Thomas O. Chisolm is noted for many hymns he has composed, but fewer are more grand than:

> Great is Thy faithfulness, O God my Father!
> There is no shadow of turning with Thee;
> Thou changest not, Thy compassions they fail
>   not:
> As thou hast been, thou forever wilt be.
>
> Great is thy faithfulness! Great is thy faithful-
>   ness!
> Morning by morning new mercies I see;
> All I have needed Thy hand hath provided—
> Great is thy faithfulness, Lord, unto me.

We sang that hymn at my son's memorial service. An anthem to the unfailing faithfulness of our God! God is a "Father of mercies" (2 Corinthians 1:3). In a variety of ways, God revealed His mercies to me. At times of stress and distress, we *need* mercy. David, the man after God's own heart, was preeminently a man of mercy. When the Lord Jesus moved about the people, as recorded routinely in Matthew's gospel, the people in need cried out, saying, "Jesus, thou son of David have mercy on us" (Matthew 9:27). The Lord never allows cries for mercy to go unheeded. During that siege of sorrow's persistence, the Lord was merciful. "Thy mercy, O Lord, is in the heavens . . ." (Psalms 36:5). I asked not only for the "mercy drops" but for showers. "Be merciful unto me, O God, be merciful unto me: for my soul trusteth in thee . . ." (Psalms 57:1). Shakespeare describes it well:

> The quality of mercy is not strain'd
> It droppeth as the gentle rain from heaven
> Upon the place beneath.

The imagery of God's word is radiant with light and warmth and love, and God marvelously and metaphorically demonstrates His mercy toward us.

> Through the days and through the nights
> Upon my bed, upon my knees
> I know no ease;
> But oh, the sights
> that Thou are pleased
> to give. These are mercy's lights.

196

The mind plays tricks when it is overwrought with sorrow's toil. God comes with dreams and visions to restore it to soundness. In the ebony world of solitude, the Lord unfolds the mystery of mercy's strength. No longer could I easily detect the thin, wavy line between dream and dull reality. "When the Lord turned again the captivity of Zion, we were like them that dream" (Psalms 126:1). I, too, felt like one dreaming, but mine was a bad dream. God sometimes reverses directions. The seeming unchangeable, God can alter. So I hoped He would reverse my son's declining health. Turn the nightmare into a dream and fill our mouths with laughter and our hearts with joy!

> Upon my bed, upon my knees
> I know no ease; these are my pleas
> that I rehearse
> that God reverse
> divine decrees.

The angel that avenged David's sin of numbering the people of Israel was sent to slay, and as the angel neared the city of Jerusalem, the peril was great. David had prayed: ". . . let me fall now into the hand of the Lord; for very great are his mercies . . ." (1 Chronicles 21:13). And the plague was stayed. At the walls of the favored city of Jerusalem, the rampage was halted and God, in mercy, spared the city. Spare, O Lord! Spare my son! The decree had been given in the hospital; like the law of the Medes and Persians (medics and physicians?), it seemed inevitable and unchangeable. But who could tell ". . . whether God will be gracious to me, that the child may live?" (2 Samuel 12:22). For "The Lord is merciful and gracious . . ."

197

(Psalms 103:8). God "... is gracious and merciful, slow to anger, and of great kindness. ... Who knoweth if he will return and repent, and leave a blessing behind him ...?" (Joel 2:13, 14). To know the character of God means knowing that God delights to be merciful, and I chose to believe that He would manifest his "tender mercies," assuredly at a time when I so desperately needed them. "Fear not ... be glad and rejoice: for the Lord will do great things" (Joel 2:21).

Isaiah came to Hezekiah and told the king his death was imminent! Straighten out your accounts, O king, your time is up! The ruler about whom the Scriptures said, "he did that which was right in the sight of the Lord, according to all that David his father did" (2 Kings 18:3) faced certain death. But Hezekiah had no heir! He, of the royal line of David, would leave no one to succeed him, and the throne would no longer hold one of David's descendants. How could God allow it? What of His covenant with David? So Hezekiah importuned God to allow him to live to sire an heir. Desperately Hezekiah prayed:

> Remember now, O lord, I beseech thee, how I have walked before thee in truth and with a perfect heart, and have done that which is good in thy sight. And Hezekiah wept sore.
>
> Isaiah 38:3

God responded favorably to Hezekiah's request. "... I have heard thy prayer, I have seen thy tears: behold, I will add unto thy days fifteen years" (Isaiah 38:5). I dared not presume to say, as did Hezekiah, that I had a perfect heart, but I prayed and wept and trusted that God would add days to my son's life. If only fifteen more so that I could see him mature and enjoy the sweet fellowship of years—the vintage of my son's ripened time. But no sundial reversed itself, and the shadow of time remained immovable.

Scripture shows God as the great restorer. "I will restore to you . . ." (Joel 2:25). Would God "restore that which he took not away"? (Psalms 69:4). As the women said to Naomi, would not someone say to me? "And he shall be unto thee a restorer of thy life . . ." (Ruth 4:15). God *could* restore Keith to health. He could reverse the deadly cancer's destruction! Through Esther's intervention, even the letter of the king was reversed (Esther 8:5–8). When we intercede, does not God delight to reverse? "When his compassion and our intercession coincide, then things begin to happen in our home," Geoffrey Bull says.[2] God can by His divine decree turn things to the contrary (Esther 9:1). God is the "repairer of the breach, The restorer of paths . . ." (Isaiah 58:12).

Through the gloom I followed the Lord. Like the Shekinah glory that overshadowed the Israelites as they journeyed through the wilderness, God's canopy of care protected me from the overwhelming terror. God was leading. The Good Shepherd "when he putteth forth his own sheep, he goeth before them, and the sheep follow him . . ." (John 10:4). And the place where He leads is "beside the still waters" and "in the paths of righteousness" (Psalms 23:2, 3) The Shepherd's crook would gently cradle me as I wandered off "astray to my own way" (Isaiah 53:6) and would return me to the fold. The rod would drive away the enemy of my soul, who would deceive me with doubts and beckon me to destruction. How comforting to feel the towering presence of the "great shepherd of the sheep," the One who was "brought again from the dead" (Hebrews 13:20). The ravenous wolves of unbelief may bay in the distance, and the scavengers of the soul may yelp during the night time of my distress, but the Shepherd who is the Chief One "shall appear" (1 Peter 5:4), and by His presence He comforts and controls.

My Joshua knew that I had "not passed this way heretofore" (Joshua 3:4), and therefore, my command was to keep some space between me and the Ark of God's presence (Joshua 3:3, 4) so I would have a clear view to see and to follow. Sometimes we need the little distance that allows a clear view to see where the Savior is leading us and we follow behind Him. And the sure word is:

> When thou passest through the waters, I will be with thee; and through the rivers, they shall not overflow thee: when thou walkest through the fire, thou shalt not be burned; neither shall the flame kindle upon thee.
>
> Isaiah 43:2

He provides a "lodging place" (Joshua 4:3, 8), and whether through the sea, through the wilderness, or through the river, He will bring us into the holy place of Canaan rest.

The place of rest is the place of God's promise. This world offers so little for the pilgrim-traveler. Infrequently we reach oases that refresh, but most often they seem only noticeable by their absence. As "strangers and pilgrims" seeking a permanent abiding place we "pitch our tents and build our altars" as did Abraham. Tents are for the transients. Altars provide the only stabilities, and these worship places always point us beyond. One day, inevitably, we "must put off this tabernacle even as our Lord Jesus Christ hath shewed us" (2 Peter 1:14), and we enter into the active rest of the full sonship of heirs of God. Our Lord's long-awaited invitation to "come unto me all ye that labour and are heavy laden, and I shall give you rest" (Matthew 11:28) affirms that serenity.

God opened the "place of quiet rest" to me. It was the secret spot—the secret place into which I was drawn to dwell. As He hid me in "the secret of his tabernacle" (Psalms 27:5) I found my soul's serenity. I once heard the eminent contemporary philosopher Mortimer Adler questioned about his belief in God. When accused of lacking warmth, Adler retorted: "It's not warmth I lack, it's rest. I lack rest." When all becomes confusion and chaos about us, how good to enter the tranquility of God's presence, where nothing clutters. Psalm 99 assures us with sublimity, that "The Lord reigneth" and that He sits "between the cherubims" and His glory covers me when I am in the "cloudy pillar," unable to see beyond the fog's fringe or in the desert's night when the fiery pillar mystifies.

From "over the mercy seat," the voice of the One who knew the cruelty of the cross speaks. The same voice spoke out of the cloud (Matthew 17:5) and out of the cloudy pillar (Psalms 99:7). This is not the voice of one crying in the wilderness, but of One who speaks from the lofty heights of heaven and whose words are those of love.

In the early days after my conversion, I would spend Sundays with other people from our church, ministering among the elderly in nursing homes in and around Philadelphia. We would hold services and preach and sing and talk to those folks. They were particularly fond of the singing and the phonograph records we played. One hymn by William O. Cushing stirred many; they were familiar with it and it touched their hearts, talking of God's *maternal* care.

> Under his wings I am safely abiding,
> Tho' the night deepens and tempest grows wild;

Still I can trust him—I know he will keep me,
He has redeemed me and I am his child.

Under his wings, under his wings,
Who from his love can sever?
Under his wings my soul shall abide,
Safely abide forever.

"He that dwelleth in the secret place of the most high shall abide under the shadow of the Almighty" (Psalms 91:1). The covert of God's care was in the security of His wingspan. Frequently I would take walks around the pond near our home, where Keith and I had once loved to stroll and talk. As we moved we would watch the annual cycle of life in the pond's waters. The ducks would lay their eggs, and the mother would brood over them and soon the fluffy yellow balls of life would hatch and faithfully follow the mother into the waters. Such unabating devotion to her ducklings became a study in maternal care and commitment. They followed close by, and when danger appeared, they snuggled under her wings, serenely content and safe. Likewise the Lord Jesus desired to gather Israel to Himself as a mother hen gathers her chicks (Matthew 23:37).

God's might shows itself in militant metaphors, and God's care shows itself in maternal metaphors. God, *El Shaddai,* is the "breasted God" who nourishes and nurtures. As I watched the ducklings on the pond, I sensed God's nurturant brooding over me just as the Spirit of God brooded over the earth at creation (Genesis 1:2). "He shall cover thee with his feathers, and under his wings shalt thou trust . . ." (Psalms 91:4). God provides these lessons throughout nature to manifest, in miniature, the tenderness of His care toward us.

As we often did, one day Keith and I were throwing the baseball back and forth on the field—a simple, unspectacular activity of which we both were fond. On one occasion a bird kept darting back and forth across the field, screeching irritatedly. She would land and dart near us, seemingly injured, and then would hobble away. At first, we thought the bird was hurt, and we wanted to help, but as we moved in her direction, she would quickly fly away. The bird would go through this routine repeatedly. Soon we realized she intended to lure us away from one particular spot, and to do this, she would pretend to have an injured wing and feign trouble. We searched the area carefully and discovered a tiny egg, lying unguarded. The mother bird had been attempting to distract us from the spot and protect her young by making us think she was wounded.

So Christ, not by pretending, but by becoming the Wounded One for us took us away from the danger of judgment and wrath. He became the bird "killed in an earthen vessel" to cleanse us from the leprosy of sin and save us from banishment from God's presence (Leviticus 14:5–7). The innocent, harmless Dove of God was made the sin sacrifice for us, and by taking the judgment Himself, justified us to God.

I mentally compared Keith's dovelike character to Christ's: my harmless and gentle boy, on whose tombstone are inscribed the words "A kind and gentle young man." That gentle youth had been ravished by cancer. The Lord Jesus Christ, dovelike innocence with no defilement, had in willing submission to His Father "been made sin for us" (2 Corinthians 5:21).

We find the place of protection under God's wings. "How excellent is thy lovingkindness, O God! therefore the children of men put their trust under the shadow of thy wings" (Psalms 36:7). When life's alarms sound fiercely and frighteningly, we can scamper beneath the outstretched wings of the "Maternal God" who lovingly gathers us around Him. His shadow is never fearsome, nor does it blot out the sun. His shadow silhouettes His presence. As the late Harry Ironsides wrote: "I'm overshadowed by his wondrous love. . . ."

The shadows of this world, foretold by the ominous clouds appearing quickly on the horizon and signaling storms, cause alarm and dismay, but when the day of Christ's appearing breaks with crystal brightness they will flee. In the words of Carl A. Blackmore's hymn:

> Some golden daybreak, Jesus will come
> Some golden daybreak, battles all won;
> He'll shout the victory, break through the blue
> Some golden daybreak for me, for you.

The shadow of the Savior comforts us, for it tells us that He towers over and is "our shield and defender," and we are able to sit "under his shadow with great delight" (Song of Solomon 2:3). The tabernacle of God, which traveled with the Israelites, symbolized God's very presence among them. God was not aloof from His people, nor had He left them alone. In my personal wilderness journey of those days, God's Shekinah presence became my constant companion. "And there shall be a tabernacle for a shadow in the daytime from the heat, and for a place of refuge and for a covert from storm and from rain" (Isaiah 4:6). The tabernacle was for a people on the move and typically that movement was "going around in circles." When it seemed that I had abandoned my senses, God did not abandon me. My mind wandered, yet the Lord "tellest my wanderings: put thou my tears into thy bottle: are they not in thy book?" (Psalms 56:8). In those days of confusion, I wrote:

> I am afraid—afraid of the *invisible* yet "seeing him who is invisible." I see outward signs of weakness

and hear symptoms of pain. Something within me does its cruel deathly work and I am powerless. I am "out of control." My soul languishes, and I (who pride myself on my ability to take charge) sit feebly by. So Lord, I trust Thee whom I fear, and I will not be afraid of frail flesh, whatever form it may take. It is *Elohim* vs. *enosh,* the Almighty vs. man.

When the soil beneath our soul seems to give way, it then reveals the Rock beneath the substratum of our frail selves. Our Lord builds only upon rock, and as Elijah met God again in the "cleft of the rock," so I sojourned to hear the "still, small voice" of comfort and consolation (1 Kings 19:12).

> . . . When my heart is overwhelmed: lead me to the rock that is higher than I. For thou has been a shelter for me, and a strong tower from the enemy. I will abide in thy tabernacle forever: I will trust in the covert of thy wings.
>
> Psalms 61:2–4

The Rock of Christ's rest is the high place from which the eternal view alone is available. "They that wait upon the Lord shall renew their strength; they shall mount up with wings as eagles . . ." (Isaiah 40:31). In the heavenly habitation, we soar *through* and then *above,* to settle in God's nest of tranquility in ethereal elevations.

> There are paths of glory that lead to worlds beyond,
> worlds of which, by faith, I'm fond
> that promise love and happiness to all who dare to turn;
> but we must learn

to soar, like the eagle and hawk;
the journey's long, and it's too far to walk.

I sat on the porch, watching the myriad of birds flitting about, wondering how God provided for them. As Jesus told us, the birds don't sow or reap, yet they are cared for. A number of sparrows settled on the street, and I watched closely to see how they would get their food. At that moment, a neighbor's door opened, and a woman threw a handful of bread crumbs, which the sparrows eagerly devoured. Sparrows, the most inconsequential of birds, and God provides for them. Swallows, the most unstable of birds are given a home in God's presence, upon His very altar (Psalms 84:3). The raven, the most insatiable of birds, at God's command shared its food with Elijah and became itself the instrument of care as Elijah was hidden away. As I was hidden away in my "cherith of bereavement"[3] God fed me with the choice morsels of His Word, and angel wings beat inaudibly as messengers came and went, unseen, in the room of my son's drought and dwindling brook.

Silence, with its golden scepter, rules in the realm of sorrow. The voiceless utterances speak most loudly when pain will not let language loose. With "groanings which cannot be uttered" (Romans 8:26) souls carry on dialogue with the Throne of Grace. Geoffrey Bull, in his solitary confinement for Christ, hidden away in the Tibetan hills, says that "the discipline of stillness was upon me in an unimagined way."[4] "Be still and know that I am God . . ." (Psalms 46:10), the Spirit speaks to a cacophonous age. As the popular song reminds us, "Tears are a language that God understands." And for rainbows, we need not have deluges, but only teardrops. The glass through which we see darkly (1 Corinthians 13:12) lets light in when it is tear-stained.

"If we walk with God in the sunlight," I would say to Keith, "then surely He will walk with us in the shadows." In God, the paternal strength and the maternal softness join perfectly. The Shepherd will not let the wolf get near the sheepcote, and He will cradle the little lamb so gently on His shoulder and near His heart. The countless ways God has chosen to describe Himself in Scripture and in experience prove His sufficiency. He does not break bruised reeds, nor does He step on broken hearts. His tender touch is the mender touch.

The four-mile course, along which I jogged almost daily, meandered lazily through country roads and tree-lined lanes and beside a gurgling brook. For part of the way, cornfields lined the sides of the road. I had witnessed, over several years, the growth of fields in the spring and summer and saw the harvest scythe reap the bounty in autumn. "While the earth remaineth," God promised Noah, "seedtime and harvest, and cold and heat, and summer and winter, and day and night shall not cease" (Genesis 8:22). The unending rhythm of nature. Through the springtime I saw the field turned over and fertilized, and soon the small shafts of green protruded above soil line. The stalks of corn sprang to life, and in the heat of summer, the ears of corn, golden yellow, seemed to burst with richness. ". . . First the blade, then the ear, after that the full corn in the ear" (Mark 4:28). The progression from seed to full growth. Then the fall, and soon they are cut down. The ground reverts to barrenness. Through the winter months, I watched the ground, snow-covered and reclusive, in sleep, awaiting the nudging sun to trigger the planting of the seed.

The summer of my son's illness, I ran seldom, but when I did, I thought: *When the harvest comes, he'll not be here! He and it will be cut down together!* The cornfield in full maturity! But my son, when he had scarcely begun to live. Reapers came for the corn harvest. Soon men had stripped the fields of their yield, and the stalks, drained and colorless, were bundled. The angels came for Keith, and his body, drained and colorless, was buried. But his spirit was carried lovingly into the presence of His Heavenly Father.

"Unless a kernel of wheat falls into the ground and dies, it abides alone, but if it dies, it brings forth much fruit" (John 12:24). Our Lord Jesus fell into the ground and died. And from that death has come the "much fruit" of the redeemed. It is axiomatic that resurrected life can only come from death. Had Adam and Eve eaten of the Tree of Life after their fall, it would have doomed them to live forever, unredeemed, in bodies of death, wasting away perpetually. Now through the Lamb's sacrifice, we have the promise of the "tree of life . . . for the healing of the nations . . ." (Revelation 22:2), and death will be banished.

On the knoll overlooking the town and countryside he loved so much, my son's body lies awaiting the last trump and the shout. The full flower of resurrected life, when soul and body reunite is the promise to all believers. Then we shall see no more planting, but *the* reaping of the harvest unto life everlasting.

> Judge not the Lord by feeble sense,
> But trust Him for His grace;
> Behind a frowning providence
> He hides a smiling face.
>
> His purposes will ripen fast,
> Unfolding every hour;
> The bud may have a bitter taste,
> But sweet will be the flower.[5]

10

Communism and Reunion

My boy, the joy had just begun
But suddenly your life is done
and stunned, I, lonely wander on
Without you, an automaton.

I wonder, dare I love again,
Or was our loving all in vain,
A passing pleasure tinged with pain?
Am I to live, or just remain?

Tormented by the nagging fear
That one, once loved, will disappear,
Should I withdraw or venture near?
Is there an answer that is clear?

"Withdraw! Withhold!" my heart replies,
"To love again would be unwise!"

Yet something whispers otherwise,
That only loving satisfies,
Beautifies or edifies.[1]

❧ 10 ❧

The greatest temptation in our lives when the dearest one we loved has gone from us is to give up. Retreat, we seek withdrawal—escape to some island of isolation on which to mourn away the days in solitude. Without hope, we desperately drift on a sea of despair, without sight of anything that is permanently fixed. *Hope* is the seed that impregnates the leaden lifelessness of the present with meaning. "Hope maketh not ashamed," Paul, the apostle of hope, reminds us (Romans 5:5). To be confounded by circumstances gone awry—to be left in a quandary is the ultimate embarrassment. *Hope* saves us from this embarrassment. It does not leave us laughingstocks when the situation of life appears as a sad comedy of errors.

Hope looks to the future. The past can provide the repository from which we draw strength and experience. It can provide the rich legacy in which God has proven Himself and where we look at Ebenezers ("hitherto hath the Lord helped us" [1 Samuel 7:12]) that testify to "grace to help in time of need" (Hebrews 4:16). But we cannot take up residence in the past. From there we have come; we cannot stay.

The future is the source of the present. Today flows from tomorrow, not from yesterday. The perspective on today must come from tomorrow's vantage point. The searchlight's beam that brightens today's spot reaches out from tomorrow's heights. Life limited to *today* for the Christian becomes misery (1 Corinthians 15:19). Today's trials can be endured, because we have the hope of tomorrow. God's assurance that our tomorrow with Him will incomparably transcend all of our todays forms the basis for our hope. Hope is not a will-o'-the-wisp that palliates the problems that bother us. Nor can it be some feathery veneer that drapes itself over the despair of death, hiding it temporarily. Hope, one of the three verities that remain (1 Corinthians 13:13), is substantial.

In his prison confinement Viktor Frankl realized survival depended upon hope. He and his fellow prisoners had to have the prospect of release and life. For us, too, the present reality demands the future hope, or the present simply becomes a prison state from which we seek to escape in whatever way we can.

> Any attempt at fighting the camp's psychopathological influence on the prisoner by psychotherapeutic or psycho-hygienic method had to aim at giving him inner strength by pointing out to him a future goal to which he could look forward. . . . It is a peculiarity of man that he can only live by looking to the future—*sub specie aeternitatis*. And this is his salvation in the most difficult moments of his existence.[2]

Major Harold Kushner, a medical army officer, was imprisoned in South Vietnam for more than five years. When he was released in 1973, he told of the horror of the conditions and the "catastrophic consequences of the loss of hope."[3] Kushner detailed the experience of a man referred to simply as Robert. Robert anticipated the prospect of release from the prison camp and cooperated with his captors. His health and state of mind were quite good, considering the privation he had suffered in the camp. When, however, Robert realized that his captors were simply "using" him and that he would not be released from the camp, he soon manifested signs of severe depression and a sense of helplessness. Eventually, Robert gave up. He wrote a brief note to his parents, and then he died. "Hope of release sustained Robert. When he gave up hope, when he believed that all his efforts had failed and would continue to fail, he died."[4]

Christians are people of hope, and Christians who have lost loved ones should be preeminently people of hope. Hope ultimately, for the believer, takes the form of "the glorious appearing of the Great God and our Savior Jesus Christ." This is, to use Paul's sublime expression, "that blessed hope" (Titus 2:13). To the sorrowing believers at Thessalonica, who had witnessed the execution and martyrdom of many saints, Paul assures them that we are not "even as others which have no hope" (1 Thessalonians 4:13). God has guaranteed that "the Lord himself shall descend from heaven . . . and the dead in Christ shall rise first" (1 Thessalonians 4:16).

Will God allow eternity to terminate what time has begun? Does not hope, by its very nature, promise the continuation, the culmination, the completion of the untidy but tangible relationships here begun? God is not some trickster who, having teased us with delights, snatches them away and leaves us empty mouthed and empty hearted. Things temporal of necessity cease to exist in temporal forms. But behind the *form* is the transcendent reality that has been and continues to be in a perfected form. He, "being in the form of God . . . took upon him the form of a servant . . ." (Philippians 2:6, 7). Forms change and are suited to the life they surround, according to the need of the life at that stage of development. Hope is inherent in every new life form. From infancy to eternity, God designs and devises forms necessary for and compatible with the life. So in eternity the relationships will flourish in resurrected life form. Geoffrey Bull describes the growth process of the life and the forms suited to it with incomparable clarity:

> The new life demands new forms and the question is, are we going to retain the old forms and squander the new life or are we going to let the new life determine everything and allow it to work out its own forms suited to its own development. . . . As the life develops, however, we find that at a certain stage this form begins to be discarded. . . . Later, however, the form again changes its appearance, and the life produces the flower. The interesting thing is that whilst the form changes and modifies yet there is a sense in which sometimes an earlier form is partly retained and runs concurrently with the later expression of the life although giving place to it. The important principle remains however, that the earlier form, although a product of the life force and essential to its expression at that stage of growth must ultimately yield to the more mature form.[5]

God's goal for His people is always maturity. The ultimate life form for believers is the resurrected life in the resurrected body. Relationships restored and renewed through the Resurrection will have the capability for the most sublime intimacies. The hope that illumines this reality assures our reunion with kindred souls in Christ. In this fundamental sense, this hope does not make us in the least ashamed.

My son in love awaits me as all heaven awaits the arrival of God's people. There is a gathering at the entrance point, and the reception is glorious, more glorious than any earthly one. The scenes with which we are familiar, as departures are common, point but weakly to the grand gathering at Glory's terminal.

The ships pulled into New York Harbor after World War II, and the massive crowds awaited loved ones long absent from these shores and from their homes. Daily travel takes one or another away, and then the happy reunion. And absence does, in God's design, make the heart grow fonder. My son's absence from me does not dull love, though there be delay. And from his unobstructed view, he, more happily than I (for he knows what awaits me) anticipates the reunion. Now we experience the hiatus, the "little while" that will reward the waiting beyond all calculation. In the interim, hope clasps the hand outstretched toward that reunion. Sheldon Vanauken, with tenderness born of intimacy, tells how he envisions it all:

> ... Davy's withdrawal towards the Mountains of Eternity—whatever it means—does not, of course, mean that I love her any the less, though it is a love without the immediacy of the flesh. Because of the dream that raised the Shining Barrier, because of the intense sharing of love and beauty, Christ and death and grief, we were perhaps as close as human

beings can be. And the union thus created will, I believe, transcend death: it endures and will endure.[6]

Grief and bereavement are no less real to God's people than
to others. In fact, the capacity for commitment in relationships
that should characterize believers in itself may cause a more
intense travail of soul when relationships end. As a people of
hope, however, we head toward the homecoming. The haven
of filial love and the magnificence of unimagined glory await
us, and they are not, as we are tempted to think, light-years
away. They are but a breath away! We cannot afford to forget,
not for a moment, that we must view present involvements
from the alpine heights and pinnacle of God's eternity and
ours. Sufferings for the present are not worthy to be compared
to (although worthy to be endured for) the everlasting glory.

> The crowning experience of all, for the homecoming
> man, is the wonderful feeling that, after all he has
> suffered, there is nothing he need fear any more—
> except his God.[7]

To that we may add, no one has or will love him more than
his God who "so loved the world, that he gave his only begotten Son, that whosoever believeth in him should not perish, but
have everlasting life."

❧ Source Notes ❧

Introduction: Loyalty's Hour

1. Dietrich Bonhoeffer, "Fortune and Calamity," *The Prayers and Poems of Dietrich Bonhoeffer,* trans. Nancy Lukens as it appeared in *Sojourners* 10 (May 1984), 25.
2. Kurt Vonnegut, Jr., *Wampeters, Foma and Granfalloons* (New York: Delta Books, 1965), 31.
3. Paul Tournier, *Creative Suffering* (New York: Harper & Row, 1983), 19.
4. Sidney J. Jourard, *The Transparent Self* (New York: D. Van Nostrand Co., 1971).
5. W. E. Sangster, "When Worn With Sickness," *He Is Able* (Grand Rapids, Mich.: Baker Book House, 1975), 18.
6. C. S. Lewis, *The Problem of Pain* (New York: Macmillan & Co., 1962), 93.

1 An Overwhelming Interference

1. A. W. Tozer, "True Faith Must Influence Our Daily Living," *Renewed Day by Day,* ed. G. B. Smith (Harrisburg, Penn.: Christian Publ., 1980), June 7.

2. C. S. Lewis, *A Grief Observed* (New York: Bantam Books, 1961), 41–43.
3. Geoffrey Bull, *God Holds the Key* (London: Pickering & Inglis, 1959), 158.
4. Joseph Bayly, "When Giving Thanks Is Impossible," *Moody Monthly* (Nov., 1976), 25.

2 Soul Sorrow

1. F. B. Meyer, *Daily Meditations,* ed. Al Bryant (Waco, Tex.: Word Books, 1979), May 10.
2. C. S. Lewis, *A Grief Observed* (New York: Bantam Books, 1961), 12.
3. William Blake, "Milton," *The Poems of William Blake,* ed., W. H. Stevenson (London: Longman-Norton, 1971), 489.
4. Lewis, *A Grief Observed,* 20.
5. Meyer, *Daily Meditations,* Nov. 1.
6. Graham Scroggie, *The Psalms* (Old Tappan, N.J.: Fleming H. Revell Co., 1965), 221–225.
7. Edward Kuhlman, "Prime Time," *HIS* (Oct., 1977), 7.
8. Meyer, *Daily Meditations,* Feb. 3.
9. I am indebted to Geoffrey Bull for this observation: Geoffrey Bull, *The Sky Is Red* (London: Pickering & Inglis, 1965).

3 Death—Thou Too Shall Die

1. John Donne, "Holy Sonnet X," *Poems of John Donne,* ed. Sir Herbert Grierson (London: Oxford Univ. Press, 1933), 297.
2. Joseph Bayly, *The Last Thing We Talk About,* rev. ed. (Elgin, Ill.: David C. Cook, 1973), 14–15.
3. C. S. Lewis, *A Grief Observed* (New York: Bantam Books, 1961), 16.

4. Robert Anderson's exegesis of this verse is helpful: Robert Anderson, *Forgotten Truths* (Grand Rapids, Mich.: Kregel Publ., 1980), 63.
5. James Stewart, *The Strong Name* (Grand Rapids, Mich.: Baker Book House, 1972), 230.
6. Lewis, *A Grief Observed*, 43.

4 My Son . . . My Son

1. C. S. Lewis, "As the Ruin Falls," *Poems,* ed. Walter Hooper (New York: Harcourt Brace Jovanovich, 1964), 109–110.
2. A. W. Tozer, *Renewed Day by Day,* ed. G. B. Smith (Harrisburg, Penn.: Christian Publ., 1980), Feb. 20.
3. David B. Biebel, "Today We Didn't Cry," *Jonathan, You Left Too Soon* (Nashville, Tenn.: Thomas Nelson, 1981), 103–111 passim.
4. C. S. Lewis, *The Four Loves* (New York: Harcourt Brace Jovanovich, 1960), 169–170.
5. Viktor Frankl, *Man's Search for Meaning* (New York: Pocket Books, 1959), 58–59.
6. C. S. Lewis, *A Grief Observed* (New York: Bantam Books, 1961), 80.
7. F. M. Lehman, "The Love of God," Nazarene Publ. House, 1945.
8. Jim Elliot, *The Journals of Jim Elliot,* ed. Elisabeth Elliot (Old Tappan, N.J.: Fleming H. Revell Co., 1978), 77.
9. Gerald Oosterveen, "Some Fathers Have to Learn That Kids Can Die Too," *Christian Living* (October, 1983), 2–4.

5 The Frozen Center of My Desert Day

1. C. S. Lewis, "Five Sonnets," *Poems,* ed. Walter Hooper (New York: Harcourt Brace Jovanovich, 1964), 125–126.
2. James Stewart, "Beyond Disillusionment to Faith," *The*

Wind of the Spirit (Nashville, Tenn.: Abingdon Press, 1968), 70.

3. Lewis B. Smedes, *How Can It Be All Right When Everything Is All Wrong* (New York: Harper & Row, 1982), ix.
4. Jim Elliot, *The Journals of Jim Elliot,* ed. Elisabeth Elliot (Old Tappan, N.J.: Fleming H. Revell Co., 1978), 91.
5. C. S. Lewis, *The Problem of Pain* (New York: Macmillan & Co., 1962), 15.
6. John Paton, *A Missionary to the New Hebrides* (New York: Fleming H. Revell Co., 1898), 130–131.

6 Fellowship of His Suffering

1. C. S. Lewis, "Love's As Warm as Tears," *Poems,* ed. Walter Hooper (New York: Harcourt Brace Jovanovich, 1964), 123–124.
2. Nikos Kazantzakis, *Report to Greco* (New York: Simon & Schuster, 1965), 483.
3. Paul Tournier, *Creative Suffering* (New York: Harper & Row, 1982), chap. 1.
4. Ian Hunter, *Malcolm Muggeridge: A Life* (Nashville, Tenn.: Thomas Nelson, 1980), 58.
5. Ibid.
6. Viktor Frankl, *Man's Search for Meaning* (New York: Pocket Books, 1959), 69–70.
7. Sheldon Vanauken, *A Severe Mercy* (New York: Harper & Row, 1977), 182.
8. *Our Daily Bread* (April 24, 1984).
9. C. S. Lewis, *A Grief Observed* (New York: Bantam Books, 1961), 28.
10. James Stewart, "God and the Fact of Suffering," *The Strong Name* (Grand Rapids, Mich.: Baker Book House, 1972), 129.

11. Lewis B. Smedes, *How Can It Be All Right When Everything Is All Wrong* (New York: Harper & Row, 1982), 56.
12. Frankl, *Man's Search*, 104–105.
13. Smedes, *How Can It Be*, 61.
14. I have developed this analogy more fully in "A Parable of the Passion," *Moody Monthly* (April, 1985).
15. Ernest Gordon, *Miracle on the River Kwai* (Wheaton, Ill.: Tyndale House, 1984), 302–303.
16. Dietrich Bonhoeffer, *The Cost of Discipleship*, rev. ed. (New York: Macmillan Pub. Co., 1963), 98–102.
17. Stewart, *Strong Name*, 147.
18. Ibid., 145.
19. Ibid., 154.
20. Ibid., 165.
21. Samuel Rutherford, *The Letters of Samuel Rutherford*, ed. Frank E. Gaebelein (Chicago: Moody Press, 1951), 20.
22. Ibid., 98.
23. Ibid., 104.
24. Ibid., 110.
25. Ibid., 114.
26. Ibid., 160.
27. Ibid., 169.
28. Ibid., 176.
29. Ibid., 116.
30. Ibid., 127.
31. Ibid., 132.
32. Ibid., 136.
33. Ibid., 190.
34. Ibid., 202.
35. Ibid., 228.
36. F. B. Meyer, *Joseph* (Fort Washington, Penn.: Christian Literature Crusade, 1975), 48.

37. A. T. Robertson, *Paul's Joy in Christ* (Grand Rapids, Mich.: Baker Book House, 1917), 108.
38. Meyer, *Joseph,* 50.
39. F. B. Meyer, *Daily Meditations,* ed. Al Bryant (Waco, Tex.: Word Books, 1979), May 17.

7 Prophets Through Pain: The Young Die

1. Calvin Miller, *The Singer* (Downers Grove, Ill.: Inter-Varsity Press, 1975), 121.
2. Nikos Kazantzakis, *Report to Greco* (New York: Simon & Schuster, 1965), 511.
3. Samuel Rutherford, *The Letters of Samuel Rutherford,* ed. Frank E. Gaebelein (Chicago: Moody Press, 1951), 209.
4. Jonathan Edwards, ed., *The Life and Diary of David Brainerd* (Chicago: Moody Press, 1949), 44.
5. Ibid., 76.
6. Ibid., 77.
7. Ibid., 79.
8. Ibid., 81.
9. Ibid., 331–333.
10. Ibid., 375.
11. Ernest Gordon, *Miracle on the River Kwai* (Wheaton, Ill.: Tyndale House, 1984), 142–144.
12. Frances Ridley Havergal, *Poems and Hymns,* ed. Tracy Bly (New Canaan, Conn.: Keats Pub. Co., 1977), 89–90.
13. Ibid., 146–147.
14. Geoffrey Bull, *The Sky Is Red* (London: Pickering & Inglis, 1965), 132–133.
15. Robert Murray McCheyne, *Memoirs of McCheyne,* ed. Andrew A. Bonar (Chicago: Moody Press, 1947), xiii.
16. Ibid., 131–132.
17. Ibid., xiv.

18. Ibid., xxvii.
19. Sally Magnusson, *The Flying Scotsman* (New York: Quartet Books, 1981), 10.
20. Ibid., 162.
21. Quoted in ibid., 162.
22. Ibid., 163–164.
23. Ibid., 169.
24. Jim Elliot, *The Journals of Jim Elliot,* ed. Elisabeth Elliot (Old Tappan, N.J.: Fleming H. Revell Co., 1978), 16.
25. Ibid., 18.
26. Ibid., 20.
27. Ibid., 50.
28. Ibid., 57.
29. Ibid., 72.
30. Ibid., 97.
31. Gordon, *River Kwai,* 145.
32. Elliot, *Journals,* 205.
33. Christian F. Gellert, "Jesus Lives and So Shall I," *The Christian Book of Mystical Verse,* ed. A. W. Tozer (Harrisburg, Penn.: Christian Publ., 1963), 120.

8   Heaven Bound

1. Frances Ridley Havergal, "Eye Hath Not Seen," *Poems and Hymns,* ed. Tracy Bly (New Canaan, Conn.: Keats Pub. Co., 1977), 188–189.
2. C. S. Lewis, *The Problem of Pain* (New York: Macmillan & Co., 1962), 147.
3. C. S. Lewis, *The Four Loves* (New York: Harcourt Brace Jovanovich, 1960), 190–191.
4. Sheldon Vanauken, *A Severe Mercy* (New York: Harper & Row, 1977), 125.

5. W. E. Sangster, *He Is Able* (Grand Rapids, Mich.: Baker Book House, 1975), 39.
6. Lewis, *Problem,* 151–152.
7. Corrie ten Boom, "Are You Going Home?" *He Cares He Comforts* (Old Tappan, N.J.: Fleming H. Revell Co., 1977), 92.

9 Metaphors of Mercy

1. C. S. Lewis, *The Pilgrim's Regress* (Grand Rapids, Mich.: Wm. B. Eerdman's Pub. Co. 1943), 144, 145.
2. Geoffrey Bull, *The Sky Is Red* (London: Pickering & Inglis, 1965), 143.
3. F. B. Meyer, *Elijah* (Fort Washington, Penn.: Christian Literature Crusade, 1978), 22.
4. Geoffrey Bull, *God Holds the Key* (London: Pickering & Inglis, 1959), 12.
5. William Cowper, "Light Shining Out of Darkness," *Masterpieces of Religious Verse,* ed. James Dalton Morrison (New York: Harper & Bros., 1948).

10 Communion and Reunion

1. David B. Biebel, *Jonathan, You Left Too Soon* (Nashville, Tenn.: Thomas Nelson, 1981), 166.
2. Viktor Frankl, *Man's Search for Meaning* (New York: Pocket Books, 1959), 115.
3. Martin Seligman, *Helplessness* (New York: W. H. Freeman & Co., 1975), 167.
4. Ibid., 167.
5. Geoffrey Bull, *God Holds the Key* (London: Pickering & Inglis, 1959), 155.
6. Sheldon Vanauken, *A Severe Mercy* (New York: Harper & Row, 1977), 232.
7. Frankl, *Man's Search,* 148.